AF740880

Spiritual Practices for Ecological Survival

RELIGION IN THE MODERN WORLD

Series Editors

Kwok Pui-lan, Emory University
Joerg Rieger, Vanderbilt University

This series explores how various religious traditions wrestle with the dynamic and changing role of religion in the modern world and examines how past changes reflect on today's critical issues. Topics address secularization, the global society, gender, race, class, sexuality, decolonialism and post-colonialism, and their relation to religious life and religious movements.

Titles in the Series:

Interrogating Religion and Peacebuilding: Global Perspectives on Power, Conflict, and Liberation edited by Jude Lal Fernando and Santiago Slabodsky
The Idolatry of Money and Human Rights by Jung Mo Sung
Liberating People, Planet, and Religion: Intersections of Ecology, Economics, and Christianity edited by Joerg Rieger and Terra Rowe
Islam in the Age of Globalization by Asif Mohiuddin
The Seven Deadly Sins of White Christian Nationalism: A Call to Action by Carter Heyward
The Hong Kong Protests and Political Theology edited by Kwok Pui-lan and Francis Ching-wah Yip
Race, Religion, and Politics: Toward Human Rights in the United States by Stephanie Y. Mitchem
Modern Muslim Theology: Engaging God and the World with Faith and Imagination by Martin Nguyen
The Politics of Jesús: A Hispanic Political Theology by Miguel A. De La Torre
The Food and Feasts of Jesus: The Original Mediterranean Diet, with Menus and Recipes by Douglas E. Neel and Joel A. Pugh
The Food and Feasts of Jesus: Inside the World of First Century Fare, with Menus and Recipes by Douglas E. Neel and Joel A. Pugh
Occupy Religion: Theology of the Multitude by Joerg Rieger and Kwok Pui-lan
Not God's People: Insiders and Outsiders in the Biblical World by Lawrence M. Wills

Spiritual Practices for Ecological Survival

Rituals of Resistance

CLÁUDIO CARVALHAES

BLOOMSBURY ACADEMIC
NEW YORK • LONDON • OXFORD • NEW DELHI • SYDNEY

BLOOMSBURY ACADEMIC
Bloomsbury Publishing Inc, 1359 Broadway, New York, NY 10018, USA
Bloomsbury Publishing Plc, 50 Bedford Square, London, WC1B 3DP, UK
Bloomsbury Publishing Ireland, 29 Earlsfort Terrace, Dublin 2, D02 AY28, Ireland

BLOOMSBURY, BLOOMSBURY ACADEMIC and the Diana logo are trademarks of Bloomsbury Publishing Plc

First published in the United States of America 2026

Copyright © Cláudio Carvalhaes, 2026

Cover design by Jen Huppert
Cover image © Marcelo Saldanha, Rio Grande do Sul, Brazil

A previous version of this manuscript was originally published in: Jeane Peracullo, Felix Roleder and Markos Jesske, eds. 2026. *Global Religion and the Climate Crisis. International Perspectives on the Relation of Religion and Nature from Practical Theology and Religious Studies.* Berlin, Boston: De Gruyter.

All figures © Marcelo Saldanha, Rio Grande do Sul, Brazil. Instagram marcelo.r.saldanha

All rights reserved. No part of this publication may be: i) reproduced or transmitted in any form, electronic or mechanical, including photocopying, recording or by means of any information storage or retrieval system without prior permission in writing from the publishers; or ii) used or reproduced in any way for the training, development or operation of artificial intelligence (AI) technologies, including generative AI technologies. The rights holders expressly reserve this publication from the text and data mining exception as per Article 4(3) of the Digital Single Market Directive (EU) 2019/790.

Bloomsbury Publishing Inc does not have any control over, or responsibility for, any third-party websites referred to or in this book. All internet addresses given in this book were correct at the time of going to press. The author and publisher regret any inconvenience caused if addresses have changed or sites have ceased to exist, but can accept no responsibility for any such changes.

A catalog record for this book is available from the Library of Congress.

ISBN: HB: 979-8-216-44938-6
PB: 979-8-216-44939-3
ePDF: 979-8-216-44941-6
eBook: 979-8-216-44940-9

Typeset by Lumina Datamatics Ltd
Printed and bound in the United States of America

For product safety related questions contact productsafety@bloomsbury.com.

To find out more about our authors and books visit www.bloomsbury.com and sign up for our newsletters.

The impossible is the place we keep returning to, time and again, when we want to change our situation. Everything we truly love was once impossible.[1]

This book is dedicated to my kids Libby, Cici, and Ike. They have changed me in more ways than they can imagine. It was because of them that I started to pay attention to the land, and from there my life was deeply transformed. This book is my way of caring for their past, their present, and their future. Also, this book is dedicated to Katie Perella-Carvalhaes for all the love and support she has always offered me. She has given me the best gift of all: to be Libby, Cici, and Ike's adopted father.

CONTENTS

LIST OF FIGURES

GRATITUDE

As I finish this book, I am incredibly grateful to so many people, human and more-than-human! Family, friends, my dog Amora, birds, squirrels, rivers, opossums, chipmunks, plants, seeds, insects, companions of all kinds, they all made this book possible. A confluence of amazing living beings! I cannot name them all. My gratitude to many generous readers, proofreaders, and writers of blurbs. Let me name just a few: my precious teacher Bonnie J. Miller-McLemore who so generously wrote the Afterword, the incredible Brazilian artist Marcelo Saldanha, who created all of the artwork for the book, Fernando Silva e Silva who has taught me most of what I know, Katy Scrogin who provided developmental editing for the book, the wonderful Series Editors, Kwok Pui-lan and Joerg Rieger, and my wonderful editor Richard Brown and also to Victoria Shi, who cared for the process of preparation of the book. To all who made this book possible, those who know it and those who never imagined, thank you! So much!

A PRELIMINARY NOTE

Toward the end of a 2019 lecture that she gave at Union Theological Seminary, Potawatomi thinker and scientist Robin Wall Kimmerer said the following:

> I would like to ask something of you. One of the things that, as I travel about, talking to people about these ideas, one of the things that I hear over and over again is a great longing from communities, a great longing to participate in ceremony, in ceremonies of grief for the earth, of ceremonies of joy for the earth, of ceremonies of commitment to the earth. And what I hear from them is this great struggle to . . . not to appropriate Indigenous earth-based ceremonies, not to borrow those ways of being. But they say, "But we don't have our own ceremonies to mourn the earth or to celebrate the earth." So in a community, a theological community where the study and practice of liturgy is so alive and well, I put that concern to you as a charge to think about this longing that I have experienced in communities wherever I go, for a ritual practice that allows people to come together around these issues. And when we think about the role of ceremony as focusing our attention so that it becomes intention, and that intention becomes action, and then the world changes. Your role in meeting that longing for ceremony can change the world. And I ask for your help in thinking about that and making it real.[2]

That night, I experienced a profound conversion that changed the course of my life. I tossed out all of my course plans and promised myself that everything I did from that day on must involve something connected to the earth. This book is an attempt to respond to Professor Kimmerer's charge to "help in thinking about that and making it real." Here, I lay out a ritual, a ceremony, to help us love the earth, to counter the devastation we are witnessing, and to build a new future for every being on the planet. If we do that, we will help the generations that come after us to live in joy, reciprocity, and gratitude. There is so much to be done—but the central belief of this book is that rituals can be a powerful force of change, a means of helping us embrace our agency and awareness. So this is a book of practice, and I follow anthropologist Jeremy Narby's understanding of practice: "Under Ashaninca influence I had come to consider that *practice was the most advanced form of theory*. I was tired of doing research. Now I wanted to act."[3]

Before we start, let me suggest three different options for proceeding with this book. *First*: if you want to focus on the details of the spiritual practice I describe, focus on "Understanding Your Bioregion: A Brief Quiz" and "Rising, Bowing, Prostrating: Spiritual Practices For a Changing Earth—An Overview." *Second*: to develop enough understanding of the practices I am asking you to engage in, you could read those two chapters along with the book's introduction and conclusion. Finally, the *third* way to approach this book is just the usual one: by reading the entire thing front to back. Every practice requires some theoretical grounding, and the book as a whole lays out important ways of thinking about and doing the rituals I describe. However you choose to read it, though, I hope the book will provide you with some means of going forward with hope and determination. Let's get started, then, rising, bowing, and prostrating ourselves with resolve.

Introduction

A chilling wind is blowing out of the Amazon rainforest, bringing disastrous news. Due to climate collapse, birds are losing body mass. The Arapaçu-bico-de-cunha and at least seventy-six other bird species are becoming smaller, their feathers displaying fewer colors—and those developments are in turn affecting their singing. As their songs change, their mating rituals grow confused, as does the entire web of relations they have with other species. The birds' very existence is compromised.[4] Their singing, their dancing, their flying: all compromised.

A timeless wisdom is rapidly being lost in a vast process of animal, plant, and soil extinction, not only in the Amazon, but all over the earth. Human wisdom, too, is disappearing at an alarming rate. The Sámi, Europe's only recognized Indigenous community, provide just one example. Having lived for thousands of years in parts of northern Scandinavia and Russia, the Sámi are losing their language and their lives as a result of environmental transformations as the Arctic "warm[s] nearly four times faster than the rest of the world."[5]

All over the globe, the rich diversity of entire biomes, made up of human and more-than-human species, is being depleted. These losses bring along with them these regions' inability to adapt and persist, and so, too, reduced possibilities for alternative futures, meaning that we also lose our past and our present.[6] At this present moment, we can't avoid the sense that the earth is falling apart. Disastrous accounts pile up of climate disasters devastating people's lives and creeping ever closer to our own doors. We all face extreme weather, growing food insecurity, the depletion of topsoil, rapid melting of icecaps, ocean warming and a massive alteration of global currents, bleaching of coral reefs, and rivers running dry. No place on earth is exempt; we are burning up!

This situation is due to our complete lack of relationship with and connection to each other and the land. As an extreme example, instead of turning to more sustainable or reasonable means of addressing population imbalances among wildlife, Alaska recently resumed the practice of shooting bears and wolves from helicopters, using the excuse that populations of caribou and moose are diminishing. But the "state's own evaluation of the practice casts doubt on its effectiveness," and the custom does nothing to improve our understanding of how bears, wolves, caribou, and humans influence each other's lives.[7]

And although we live as if infinite resources were available for our use, the earth cannot support such voracity. We live and move within particular environments, ignorant of their unique laws and patterns, unaware of how we must change our own routines and expectations if we humans and more than humans will be able to survive and thrive well into the future. Our consumption-focused lifestyles take no heed of scientific warnings about climate change. And while all species are negatively impacted by these circumstances, it is a comparatively small portion of humans who account for an outsize use of global resources. It is the rich countries, the most industrialized, who are the world's worst polluters, emitting the largest amount of greenhouse gases (GHGs). To be more specific, the problem lies in the hands of the ten percent of the human population who are constantly stealing, hoarding, abusing, and swallowing the earth for their own pleasures and benefits, holding a capitalist gun to our heads.[8]

It seems that things are only getting worse. Across the globe, countries are unwilling to change their understanding of the earth. Capitalism is ubiquitous, and has forced every nation to operate according to a demanding economic mindset that views everything we do and all we are through the lens of economic growth, development, and progress. A truly alarming—desperately alarming—situation!

But we can't just give in to despair or a sense of powerlessness. Instead of shrugging and watching as the world erodes before our very eyes, we must get up and do something, even if it feels like trying not to fall off a crumbling mountain. Together, we must hold onto the mountain—and hold the mountain together—for as long as we can. For we are responsible not only for the mountain but also for past generations who cared for it, and for future generations who will depend on that mountain to survive.

What is left, though, for individuals to do? How can those of us in search of some form of action and connection respond to this apocalypse? Ayana Elizabeth Johnson gives us a hint:

> Now what can a regular person do to push cities and states to fill the growing federal void? A lot... let's focus on just one key action: Join a local environmental group. In other words, find a home, a community, for your planet-protecting, life-sustaining work, and settle in for the long haul. This is no trite step. In the words of Bill McKibben, climate journalist and activist, "Faced with the kind of crises that we face, the most important thing that an individual can do is to not always be an individual."[9]

We can no longer consider ourselves "individuals." In other words, we cannot understand ourselves as discrete, autonomous beings, finding our grounding in our own individual will and freedom. Our living is not an individual task, our learning is collective, our existence depends on others. Our healing is collective, and our accomplishments happen because of a village. None of us is, nor have we ever been, only "one." Each of us is always many, always already plural. We can no longer be certain, in fact, about who an *I* really is. That *I*, that self, we strive so desperately to know, is the most opaque being there is. Hardly something we can claim as a ground or source. As Gil Anidjar recently declared, "I can never say I was born. Rather that I was given birth by my mother."[10]

Our sense of being in the world must then be collective, understanding people, rivers, trees, birds, animals, and plants as fundamental parts of oneself, a self living in connected but simultaneously distinct and plural worlds. That is our richness, our collective bio-cultural-natural-social species diversity. As a recent popular saying has it in Brazil, "We are not defending nature; we are nature defending itself."[11]

It's true: many of us are weighed down by the sense that everything is changing. The certainties that have shaped our lives for so long are disappearing. War, destruction, brutality; chemical and nuclear weapons; the known and as-yet unknown harms of AI: they oppress us all. As we exhaust the earth, bombs continue to explode over Gaza and so many other parts of the world—and as our world crumbles, we can do nothing but love it. It is what we have; it is who we are. As the earth burns, new possibilities may arise; the ruins we are left with may be a sign of new beginnings. But as Spanish writer and philosopher Paul Preciado reminds us, "We are not mere witnesses of what is happening. We are the bodies through which mutation arrives and takes place. The question is no longer who we are, but who (or rather what) we are going to become."[12]

CHAPTER ONE

Rising, Bowing, Prostrating

Spiritual Practices for a Changing Earth—An Overview

Wherever you stand, be the Soul of that place.

RUMI

Let's start with an overview of the three-part liturgical gesture I ask my students to make every day, three times a day. Although they are welcome to engage in the movements at different times of the day, I suggest they do so when they wake up in the morning, before or after lunch at midday, and before going to bed in the evening. While this gesture is intended for individuals, it can be very enriching to do as a collective practice that includes each individual sharing with the others how it has affected them. You can do these movements in your room, in your backyard, next to the tree in front of your house, in the local park, next to the nearby river, when you hear a bird or spot a opossum, on your daily walk, whenever you happen to look up, in a forest, at your farmers market, in a religious setting, at a crossroads, in a gathering of friends, at a street demonstration, or during political protests. In other words, anywhere! The gesture is intended as a spiritual tool to help you move through the many disasters and crises we are currently facing.

But before we get into the details, let me offer a note about the ritual's adaptability across religious traditions. You'll notice that the gesture as I lay it out is offered from a Christian perspective, framed by Jewish scriptures and the Gospels. Please frame and reframe the ritual with your own sacred scriptures, your own sources of wisdom and spirit.

The liturgical act entails a bodily prayer in three gestures: *rising*, *bowing*, and *prostrating*. These gestures and words compose the breath of our living and our hopes of mirroring our deepest relationships with everything around us: when we *rise*, we pay attention to the skies, to treetops and mountaintops and beyond, where the ozone layer makes our climate livable. When we *bow*, we greet everyone around us: people, animals, plants, water. When we *prostrate* ourselves, we touch the ground; we reconnect with the earth, the soil, humus, and the subterranean world.

The gestures can be adapted to every body type and ability. While rising, bowing, and prostrating are central to this particular ritual, readers live with different forms of embodiment and disability, and should move and perceive their bodies according to their individual gifts and limitations. Rising, bowing, and prostrating are about multiple means of engaging with—not just adapting to—the body and its vast possibilities, and everyone is welcome to enact the ritual according to ability, desire, and need.

*

Rising. For this first gesture—your welcoming morning prayer—stand, or raise any part of your body to the skies above you. If you are able, raise your arms as far as they will go and your head to the skies, offering a prayer of gratitude, glory, and celebration. If you can't see the skies or come up with a prayer, let your heart speak in silence. Remember that your origins are grounded in stardust, and that infinite universes far beyond our own are living and thriving!

If you are struggling with a particular situation, conflict, or trouble, put one leg, arm, or any other part of your body forward as if in fighting mode. Stretch your arms and head forward. This is your warrior stance. Open your eyes, ears, and hands wide; bare your teeth, say what you have to say, rebuke what needs to be rebuked, curse what needs to be cursed, push away what needs to be pushed away, open your hands, and say to your troubles that they are not allowed here.

According to your ability, raise any part of your body; you could be standing, seated in a chair, or lying in your bed. Move your toes, incline your head gently, or think of getting up. Stay in that position for a while until you feel your body connect with the air, the skies, the birds, the sounds of the place. Remember to listen to every sound around you, smell the local smells, touch what you can touch, taste what you can taste, and imagine the spirits of the place receiving you. Offer a few words to the Spirit and/or spirits (you can name your own forms of relation here) around you. Slowly inhale and exhale five times. Each time, you can repeat your original words, come up with new ones, or just remain silent.

*

Bowing. For the second gesture, bend forward in a posture of respect. Bow to what is around you. Look around, and to each being you see, offer a word of gratitude. If you encounter a dead tree, say a prayer of gratitude for this tree. If there is a bird on the ground, bow and thank the earth for the life of this precious being. If possible—and only with gloves or other means of protection—bury or relocate the body and provide it a funeral. If the land before you has been devastated, bow and remind yourself and the space of the precious presence of those who were once there, humans and nonhumans.

After thoroughly studying your surroundings, bow and let your eyes meet the floor. You can let your arms hang to the floor, or you can raise them alongside your body to any degree. You can also place your hands over your heart, holding it as you pray. Speak, sign, write a word of celebration for all that is and is coming, and a word of sorrow for all that has been taken away, ripped apart, destroyed. Stay like that for a few seconds and let your heart feel the space around you. In this gesture, you are also holding the earth's pain and sorrows; you are holding the earth with love. Tell the earth you care for her, that you are carrying her sadness, and that you want to heal her wounds. As you did when bowing, remember to listen to every sound around you, smell the local smells, touch what you can touch, taste what you can taste, and imagine the spirits of the place receiving you. Offer a few words of gratitude to the Spirit and/or the spirits (you can name your own forms of relation here) around you. Slowly inhale and exhale five times. Each time, you can repeat your original words, come up with new ones, or just remain silent.

*

Prostrating. For the third gesture, if possible, prostrate yourself, placing your forehead on the ground. Feel your entire body connecting with the earth. You might kneel or sit on the floor or in the grass, or focus on your feet or chair or bed standing on a firm foundation, or even imagine touching your forehead to the soil—whatever you choose, always keep your heart alert. Feel the earth in the palm of your hands and on your head and knees. Say a word of gratitude for the land who gently receives you. Let all your pain and mourning and sadness go into the ground: the earth will receive all your tears and sustain your body. Remember you are dust; you came from the soil and to the soil you shall return. Remember the earth is holding you with care and love.

Remember where you come from; remember your ancestors and all who have made a way out of no way for you. Whatever your gender, color, sex, or religion, be grateful: a great diversity of people has helped you come this far. Again, remember to listen to every sound around you, smell the local smells, touch what you can touch, taste what you can taste, and imagine the spirits of the place receiving you. Use multiple forms of bodily engagement to experience the place around you. Offer a few words of gratitude to the Spirit and/or the spirits (you can name your own forms of relation here) around you. While kneeling or prostrate, slowly inhale and exhale five times. Each time, you can repeat your original words, come up with new ones, or just remain silent.

*

We must start each gesture with gratitude and the feelings associated with that particular movement. So when we rise, we express gratitude for all that is above us and signal the courage to keep living, offering a sign of defiance against whatever wants to push us down; of strength to rise in body and spirit against the forces of death; and of power, knowing that yes, we can change things! When we bow, we speak a word of gratitude to everything around us and mourn everything that is dying or has died. We name those who are in pain, animals being extinguished, plants that produce our oxygen, seas and rivers who are dying, and biomes endangered by climate change. And when we prostrate ourselves, making contact with the ground, we offer a word of gratitude for subterranean life and for everything that springs forth from below: water and seeds and everything essential for life's fullness. When we touch the ground, we reconnect to our humus, humility, the core of our being.

With every posture, feel the Spirit of the land coming to you. The Great Spirit is all around you; call and hear what the spirit(s) is/are saying. Wherever you stand, bow, or lie, the Spirit is at home, and you must connect with the vibrancy and liveness of everything that surrounds you. The Spirit is not an idea, not only a feeling; it is the presence of all life, in every single being around you. How can you connect with all that fullness of life?

*

In the beginning, it is important that you envision yourself engaging in the motions, moving your body according to your limitations and abilities along with the environment, as the environment. Start to consider how you can keep this prayer going and expand upon its words, thoughts, feelings, postures, and connections. This gesture is a prayer, a way of relating with everyone around us and deep within us. This gesture is a performance, not in the sense of something fake or false, as if simply making a wish or pretending we believe or trying to become spiritual-not-religious. None of that! As a performance, prayer is an action that produces an effect, entails a process, enters into a relation, engenders responses, and creates forms of consciousness—or as ritual theorist Catherine Bell describes performance,

> our terms are best used as a minimalist set of props with which we can begin to engage ideas and inquire into practices that may well modify the surroundings. If performance terminology can evoke this type of open stage as well as it has evoked the dramatic fullness of human actions, it will continue to be a vital asset in modern discourse on religion.[13]

This means that my suggested one-act performance in three gestures provides a minimalist set of props that allows us to experience the fullness of life in a spiritual mode. The liturgical is thus an enactment of balance in a world that is unbalanced by forces of death and by energies leading us to destruction. This ritual opens up a world stage by evoking our belonging in and through relationships—balancing death with life! These liturgical spiritual gestures, then, embrace nothing less than the whole world, where the possibility of life's fullness is a matter not only for the human species but for *every* living species. Too much in our lives and the world is unbalanced, and these gestures aim for a continual restoration of balance, so that life and death, pain and wellness, in the human, animal, vegetal, and water-filled worlds are continuously brought into a certain proportion that will allow all life to flourish fully. This prayer is thus a way of understanding our own human world and of opening up spaces for the worlds of every species on earth.

In the following sections, we will go into detail about the meaning and movement of each gesture. But I will first close this introduction with music, which often helps rituals to flow. I have composed the song below to carry us through each gesture. You are invited to learn and sing it as you move, even following along online if desired.[14] You can also substitute for my use of "earth" the source of life you associate with most closely, whether God, the Dharma, Allah, Jesus, the Great Spirit, or others.

To the skies I rise
To the earth I bow
To the ground I touch
In the earth I rest

Filling out the gestures

We have learned the basics of each gesture—but let's look at each in more detail.

Rising

We have to remind ourselves that we must rise all the time!

In a world that is always trying to crush us and put us down, to rise is an act of both resistance and defiance, an act of solidarity with those who are struggling. Rising is a spiritual gesture that reaches out for strength, reenvisioning, and sustenance. Although society is so often expert at putting us down, time and again we must rise. As we fight against fascism, climate destruction, nationalisms, and more, we must know where to find sustenance. Remember Psalm 121, when the Psalmist said in despair:

> I lift up my eyes to the hills—
> from where will my help come?
> My help comes from God,
> who made heaven and earth.

When we lift up our eyes, we find that sustenance; we are able to rise, to elevate ourselves above surrounding circumstances and prevail, even when we are defeated. We learn to rise with Black communities, who developed the notion of elevation over a century ago. As theologian Gayraud S. Wilmore says,

> The concept of "elevation" appears, by the wide use of that very word, to be well established in African American literature throughout the nineteenth century. Black men and women, clergy and lay, envisioned a broad horizon of racial uplift and advancement through religion. They were the people who dominated the free black communities of the North and the major cities of the South, when they could get away with it, to lead such causes as seeking opportunities for higher education for their children, the boycotting of goods produced by slave labor, resistance to efforts of the American Colonization Society to return them to Africa, and the promotion of moral reform, lyceums, and benevolent societies.[15]

Here, elevation *is* the work of rising up together, as a collective. We could even say that Black history is one of fully fledged elevation, the constant creation of countless forms of mutual uplift. As the title of what is known as the Black National Anthem has it, "Lift every voice and sing."[16] The song is a way of being in the world: of rising, sustaining, standing up to the challenges of the day, and when possible, staying alive. With a long history of struggle against endless attempts to crush them, Black communities knew and are still well aware of the need for elevation.

> To the skies I rise
> To the earth I bow
> To the ground I touch
> In the earth I rest

Bowing

Bowing is the second gesture in our liturgical ritual. To bow means to recognize the fullness of presence in everything. We bow down to the presence of every human being, every plant, every mountain, every animal, every insect, every body of water, be it a cloud, a small river, or an ocean! To bow means to recognize those among us who have been stripped of their humanity. It means to bow to others and even to ourselves. It is to commit our love to and work for and with them. Each being carries the spirit of life and the Spirit of the earth.

To bow down is to offer a sign of humility, of understanding that we are no greater than the squirrel running in our backyard, the birds singing around us, the rivers flowing near our homes, the plants around us. Every single being bears the fullness of presence, and we bow down to each as we tell them: I wish you happiness, peace and protection.

Bowing down means getting in touch with all the world's hurt, including our own; it means giving ourselves to all beings' sorrows and pain. We weep with those who have been incarcerated, with dying lands and rivers, with animals slaughtered, with so many species nearing extinction. When we bow, we say to them all: I hear you; I grieve for all who live in poverty, for all who have been killed, destroyed, brutalized, murdered. We bow down and we weep with and for them. To bow down is to look at the pain in front of and around us. By bowing to every single being we commit fully to the life and the death of each being.

I invite you now to bow down and silently say the names of those in need of mercy, kindness, healing, love, and life. To bow to people and other-than-human beings in need of honor, deliverance, freedom, and sustenance. It may even be that you are the one who needs to hear that from yourself.

To the skies I rise
To the earth I bow
To the ground I touch
In the earth I rest

Prostrating

Prostration is an act of reconnection, regaining the connection we have lost with the land. For the most part, we go about our lives never paying attention to the earth, to birdsong, to the sprouting of seeds; we give no thought to where our food comes from, to the all-important pollinating activity of bees. We know nothing about the realities of any other beings. We have forgotten that we are enmeshed in the fullness of the earth, that our tiny bodies are part of a much larger skin, the body of the earth. Bruno

Latour, a French philosopher, would say that we live as if we have never landed on earth.[17]

In fact, our daily lives often depend upon practices of dominion and power—transportation and shipping that rely on fossil fuels, agribusiness that destroys native ecologies, energy-intensive processes of data transfer and sharing—that lead to famine, extinction, and the inability to live and survive in our own places. We need to return to the ground, to the soil we came from, and realize we are nothing but that soil, that humus. From dust, we came and to dust we shall return. In prostrating ourselves, we connect again with God as we reconnect with the earth.

In African religions, the head is fundamental to determining the orientation of the cosmos. And the head has to touch the ground. Many other traditions follow this instruction to place one's head on the ground. For example, in the rites of ordination followed by the Episcopal and Roman Catholic Churches, the ordinant must lay their entire body on the floor. And Buddhist and Muslim prayers and rituals often involve prostration.

With our head on the ground, then, we remember we are of the earth, and we rediscover our belonging and our strength. With our head on the ground, we understand that the soil needs better care, better tending, just as all of us also need better care and tending. With our head on the ground, we learn that the earth is the bearer of our history, history that is collected and compacted in layers of sediment—and so we cannot allow what has been there for ages to be removed and burned as fossil fuel. With our head on the ground, we realize that our God is mud and from the mud come our spirit and our stories, the lore of our lives, our collective stories of plants, animals, and humans. Prostrating ourselves with our heads on the ground, our hearts fly to the sky, forming a bridge between heaven and earth. Connected—fully connected!

Bringing the gestures together

Where were you born? Using a compass, turn in the direction of the place where you arrived in the world. This is the place where you were wonderfully and fearfully made. At that place, stardust from our universe and even others found its way onto that piece of land, that neighborhood, and composed your body and heart; even the Milky Way is within you! It was where your Spirit first breathed in this world. Star particles joined with the flowing waters, the moving air, the sparkling fire, and soil that only emerged after eons, all contributing to the perfect climate that allowed you to take this particular form of being. When you arrived in this place, you joined billions of other sentient beings, continuing together to shape this earth. It is as if this territory had given you the largest possible measure of your own subjectivity, a full sense of self that can only be experienced in relationship. When you reconnect your soul with the place of your birth, you are visited by past generations, the cloud of witnesses now becomes the soil, the mud in which they now live. Thus, your ancestors and those of others greet you right where you are, reminding you of countless others who came before you in that place. And all of a sudden, realizing the powerful ways that heaven meets the earth, we must walk slowly.

Look down now at your feet and connect with where you are. Feel the ground beneath you and sense how you are united with the place where your body, heart, and soul are found in this moment, where you breathe the breath of life. Touch this ground very softly; you are in a place that was sacred to many other beings who were here before you.

Now if you can, prostrate yourself. (If you are unable, put your head in your hands and feel your feet in contact with the ground.) Place your head on the earth and let your heart fly to the skies. Now you belong to this place—honor it! Put your ear to the ground and listen to the earth: what are other beings telling you? While listening in this way, remind yourself of the soil you are made of and the breath God has blown into your body to give you the gift of life. Pray for the earth and its wellbeing; pray for all who live upon and in it.

To the skies I rise
To the earth I bow
To the ground I touch
In the earth I rest

Conclusion

When we engage in this ritual, we are learning *to rise* above circumstances and connecting with everything above us. When we *bow* to every being around us, we honor them all; and when we *touch* the ground or *prostrate* ourselves, we are beginning to become again who we are: the land. On your own or with others, practice these gestures every day or every time you can.

FIGURE 1 *The harvest of devastation.*

CHAPTER TWO

Counteracting a 500-Year-Old Gesture

A New Spirit

The first living being to die with the arrival of the colonizers in Brazil was a *tree*. When the Portuguese arrived in 1500, the first thing they did was to cut down a tree to make a cross to celebrate a mass.[18] This first gesture performed in the New World at the very beginning of the era of colonization was in fact a liturgical ritual, one that preannounced the killing of 56 million Indigenous people and the devastation of the land. That liturgical gesture has encompassed countless ways of still-continuous colonization, murder, and devastation of people and the land. That gesture has grown and spread, leading to the entire global economy's thorough organization around the full-scale extraction of the earth's very life: what we often refer to as earth's resources. Here, the natural world is assumed to have no value beyond its valuation as capital—an attitude that is ultimately responsible for climate disaster.

The liturgical ritual this book offers is one done in three gestures, namely rising, bowing, and prostration. This ritual is intended as a practice of resistance to that earlier colonial gesture. Instead of killing a tree, it hopes to instill in us a love of trees and everything about the land, starting from our own local landscapes. In this way, this gesture wants to counter, symbolically, and hopefully concretely, the ongoing colonial, capitalist, fascist project of death and horror. This liturgical gesture offers a way to reimagine new forms of living, hopefully leaving something behind for generations to come. We move from the first gesture of killing a tree to rising, bowing, and prostrating to everything that is around us. From the legacy of a colonial act, we transition into other ways of caring for the earth by beginning to invent new forms of relation and reconnection with the landscapes we live in.

We also need a new spirit that will transition us out of colonial time and space into a new place and time, for the spirit that guides our mode of living is leading us to a dead end. That spirit is disconnecting us from the land and reorienting our belonging to things that cannot last: to hoarded stuff! This spirit has taken our hearts and minds, leaving us with nothing but fear, anxiety, and sadness. We are always running, always struggling against someone else to hold onto a place where we can survive on our own. We have lost the sense of belonging to a village where everyone takes care of everyone else.

We need a large-scale response; of course we do. Of course, we must be part of environmental movements that understand the natural world is related to the political realm and to racial, gender, and class struggles, all of which are related to each other. Only then will we be able to confront the problems occurring within our own bioregions.[19] We are living out so many crises together: ecological, political, social, epistemic, educational, economic, and religious crises; crises of immigration and movement of refugees, of food sovereignty, morality, and so on. I am calling the combination of all these crises a spiritual crisis. Because there is one spirit at the center of it all, destroying everything everywhere: the spirit of capitalism.

This idea will be developed in a later part of the book—but suffice it to say that the spirit of our time is the spirit of capitalism, which devours everything without measure or thought of consequence. Capitalism is what orients our relationship to the land, our relations with one another; it is what guides our jobs and tells us who we should help live and who is disposable, left to die. Capitalism instills in us the feeling that directs us to compete with one another. It tells me that you are the enemy, the foe to be destroyed if I am to survive. Capitalism shows us how we must be in the world: I must work hard if I am to be included; otherwise, my exclusion means nobody will care for me. Capitalism removes from our vocabulary the words care and solidarity, replacing them with competition and individual strength. Today's religious maxim is God is for me and against everyone else.

That spirit teaches me that the human need for private wealth is real. Private property becomes my place of safety and security in a world where everyone is out to get as much as they can. I must do everything I can, then, to increase my personal gain even if it means someone else must live with less: a game, perhaps a hunger game, and I must survive at all costs. We all know what the end result is: mass destruction. These are the means and these are the results of the spirit of capitalism orienting the very core of our being.

That spirit orients our forms of living and demands racial and caste distinctions. The imposition of white supremacy is the condition of that spirit's continuing life. The whiteness of that spirit feeds on the breath of nonwhite folks. But it also crushes poor whites. That spirit is sustained by patriarchy and heterosexism. That spirit is the spirit of brutalism, which crushes queer people, women, children, and the poor. This spirit works with any religion that will support its appetite for crushing and devouring and killing everything.

That spirit is the breath of fascism, the creator of safe rooms that shelter some white people while the rest of the world burns and dies. That spirit depends upon a perpetually economic understanding of global issues, placing the earth in the margins of history. Indian historian Dipesh Chakrabarty contends in *The Climate of History in a Planetary Age* that climate change demands we adopt a different historical structure.[20] We cannot think or act according to a framework that assumes humans are the world's most important actors, that human value is the only criterium for the wellbeing of nations. Instead, Chakrabarty says that we must cultivate a broader understanding, so that our thought embraces a planetary structure in which humans are decentered and geological, biological, geographic, and climatological issues are addressed. In this way, Chakrabarty pushes against the spirit of our time, which is concentrated on global (human) trade, economic development, growth rates, and so on as the only valid measurements of our wellbeing. That spirit is killing us.

It is because of the strength of that spirit that we must offer another spirit to replace it. Only spiritual practice can actually respond to all of these crises. A spiritual practice that engages *with* other ones and an-other, both humans and more-than-human species. We need a spiritual practice that can teach us to breathe differently, in relation, that can keep our hearts alive, our bodies connected, and our minds engaged. A spiritual practice that can help us find accompaniment, not only with other people but also with trees, rivers, birds, squirrels, opossums, whales, jaguars, coral reefs, and countless others.

CHAPTER THREE

The Spiritual Practices

We need to create new spiritual practices that can work to put a stop on these ongoing colonial practices. We start with these spiritual practices to first and foremost help us engage with the natural world, the land we are inhabiting; that is, the environment we are fundamentally a part of. This spiritual practice must start with a simple set of movements that will bring us to the realization that we are not, again, discrete individuals, but collective beings living with other collective beings around us. This spiritual practice is the enactment of a three-part gesture, a ritual movement that anyone can do and that, with time, can hopefully replace the spirit of capitalism with the spirit of the land. As we continue to carry it out, this practice can spark different forms of doing, feeling, and living, ushering in different forms of relationship and transformation, both inward and outward. It is a ritual that can help us change our perceptions, reconfigure our imagination, stir up our sense of connection and belonging. A ritual that can remind us that we have no future—only the present—and only by living fully in the present might a possible future emerge.

This practice entails three mo(ve)ments. (1) It starts with the individual, granted that we understand from the very beginning that the individual is not a discrete self but a collective, a gathering, a social composition with the land. The I, that is always a we, by hearing a certain call from the land, activates our earth memory, and we move our bodies toward that call. As we hear it, we feel a little disquiet, a lack of something so integral to us, a loss of something we know so well. This call ignites a mix of a desire to do something and at the same time a sense of powerlessness, not knowing what this call fully is, not knowing what to do. Yet, you and I decide to do something. We open a place within us for a desire to connect with the land, to be awakened, and to be cherished. You and I, each one of us a collective since we are so many other beings within ourselves and around us, as we depend on a number of other beings, we begin to do these ritual practices and begin paying attention to the places we live, relating with the beings who are right there with us. (2) Then our *individual/collective* actions join others in a collective mo(ve)ment of actions where we live. Each person desiring to connect with a different patch of land, and all of us connected with something for the wellbeing of the land. Together, we create neighborhood associations, we join other groups who are already doing the work that needs to be done. Some of us will care for the birds, some will care for the soil, and we all will take care of the river near us. (3) Then the third mo(ve) ment happens when we start to make our collective actions become more clearly political decisions to change the ways and the laws we live socially in a village, a town, a city, a state, a country. We join/create organizations that will press politicians and governments to change the way we live. We will prohibit companies from dumping poisonous materials in the river, we will orient our homes to turn off the lights during bird migration, we will stop the disposal of toxins onto the land, we will depend on local produce and incentivize supporting the local economy. Supporting the life and wellbeing of all beings around us. Humans and more than humans are what will orient our eco-nomos, that is, our economy, and not the other way around. In this way, we will imagine a new life together!

These gestures form a ritual and that is what we are intending here, to restore rituals of relation, of connection, of mutual belonging, reciprocity and care with the places live. Rituals that can help us turn foreign places into home, oikos. The notion of rituals here is very close to what Robin Wall Kimmerer calls Indigenous ceremonies. She describes ceremonies in this beautiful way:

> Ceremonies large and small have the power to focus attention to a way of living awake in the world. The visible became invisible, merging with the soil . . . The land knows you, even when you are lost . . . Ceremony is a vehicle for belonging—to a family, to a people, and to the land. . . . That, I think, is the power of ceremony: it marries the mundane to the sacred. The water turns to wine, the coffee to a prayer. The material and the spiritual mingle like grounds mingled with humus, transformed like steam rising from a mug into the morning mist. What else can you offer the earth, which has everything? What else can you give but something of yourself? A homemade ceremony, a ceremony that makes a home.[21]

This sense of ceremony that is so embedded in her people, the Potawatomi Nation, is also perceived in her father's morning coffee ritual while camping. When he poured the first coffee of the day onto the ground, it was an offering to the land and to the spirit/Spirit/s of the land: "Here's to the gods of Tahawus."[22]

This small gesture carried a deep relation to the land everywhere he went. This book wants to help us connect our small gestures where we live with much larger forms of feeling, thinking, desiring, and relating. The gestures in this ritual hope to result in practices that actually do something more to us and everybody around us. That is why it must be grounded in an individual/collective sense of belonging. If we think that pouring a cup of coffee onto the land will do the trick, and we finally say to ourselves "I got it" and keep believing we can do anything alone, we have been captured by the spirit of capitalism and we will continue devouring the earth. For that cup of coffee poured onto the land was a result of a heart already involved with a way of being in the world.

In this way, if this practice gets stuck with the individual only, it will not be sustained. It will be just another greenwashing dispositive of capitalism that will continue feeding the system that is destroying us. We can't turn this book into yet another individualistic practice, a self-help book that will say: Do this and you will be satisfied, happy now with nature. This book hopes to do something completely different. In fact, the practice I am describing is fundamentally opposed to self-contentment. These gestures are not about being happy by learning how to relate to the earth, even if we seek a certain experience of bliss. Rather, these ritual gestures are fundamentally an attempt to ignite forms of mutual restoration. If we are able to do that then happiness will be a consequence we will realize later. If we can engage in forms of mutual healing and restoration, then people, animals, flowers, rivers, forests, we will all be happy!

These practices hope to reorient our beings back to the land, and since we are the earth, these practices will help us remember who we are, and who we have always been. Then we will realize that our lives will be amplified, intensified. As Belgian philosopher of science Vinciane Despret described so beautifully the very core of each earthling:

> Each living being is guided, throughout life, by an insatiable creative drive. This drive can take diverse forms. Thus, at the most elementary level, each living being is, inextricably, a condition of existence for other living beings, which are themselves conditions of their own existence—including by the fact of dying and feeding other living beings. Each living being is, therefore, in fact, the bearer of an ontological responsibility that it will be forced to assume, and that at times it will even insist on assuming. The more a living being assumes this responsibility, the more its existence will be amplified, intensified. In other words, each living being receives its own "intensity of existence" by giving it to others and receiving it from others.[23]

As we carry each other's possibilities of life, we must be aware of that which breaks these patterns and destroys these connections. That is why this book is both an encouragement of earthling self-awareness (as a collective) and a call for a revolution and the undermining of capitalism.

That is why it is very important to remember that these practices, as shared technologies of the self, as means of producing who we are and can become, are inextricably connected with capitalism. Capitalism has a *spirit*, which is a way of breaking the collective into the individual, a mode of production, a set of practices that ties us to certain affections, beliefs (religious or not), desires, ways of thinking that orient our forms of paying attention, of doing, of being, of relating. That Spirit is collective but works within ourselves. Said in another way, capitalist power operates not just through external coercion or ideological mystification, but by embedding itself in the very production of subjectivity itself—in how we perceive, feel, think, and desire. Philosopher Felix Guattari makes it clear when he says:

> To the traditional means of direct coercion, capitalist power continually adds control devices that require, if not the complicity of each individual, at least their passive consent . . . It is in the basic functioning of perceptual, sensitive, affective, cognitive, linguistic behaviors, etc., that the capitalistic machinery embeds itself, whose deterritorialized "invisible" part is, without doubt, the most implacably effective. We cannot accept theoretical explanations of the subjectification/subjugation of the masses based on some kind of ideological trickery or collective masochistic passion. Capitalism seizes human beings from within. . . . Individuals are "equipped" with modes of perception or the normalization of desire, in the same way as factories, schools, and territories.[24]

This book intends to help us see how caught we are in this system of perception, of desire, of living in a mode of sheer consumerism, of buying, of profit, of making everything private property. We do this with our own subjectivity, our bodies and the land around us.

Much of our disconnection from the earth has to do with the way capitalism makes us view nature as a resource for development and profit. Here, the natural world doesn't have a life or a value of its own, but consists instead of "empty" spaces of forests, rivers, and biomes that are waiting to be developed and produce a profit, whether through buildings, factories, or extraction of riches and many forms of life called simply "resources." The practices described in this book aim at the transformation of these forms of capitalist relations with the land, and it is only collectively that we can achieve that transformation. These practices intend to create transformative collectives that work ultimately to do away with capitalist systems, values, and organizations. These technologies of the self aim to create a different self, not the present one designed for a world in which each individual must fight for itself and against others. Instead, rising, bowing, and touching the ground intend to bring forth another spirit/Spirit/s, to be found in ourselves and in the land. It is then this spirit/Spirit/s that will be able to undo the capitalist spirit by breaking capitalist patterns and reorienting our desires, habits, and attention. These practices hope to recreate a collective self that understands we belong fundamentally to the earth, to each other, and to all the species around us. That is our ontological responsibility.

These are practices of reimagination. We are constantly pushed to follow the market and do what it takes to achieve the best position, the highest-paid job, to be entrepreneurs of the self. This is not at all what I am proposing here. What I offer instead is the possibility to slow down, so that we can perceive the land's own slow-moving processes. These practices are ways of reimagining oneself as a collective, and to do that, we need a community, a church, a neighborhood association, or some group form. Community is fundamental to connection, for although we are bombarded with tales of individual accomplishment, there is a limit to what any individual can offer or do on their own. The practice's aim is captured well by a supposedly African saying: "If you want to go fast, go alone; if you want to go far, go together."[25] In changing the way we live, our work of imagination involves inventing a new, and simultaneously old, way of living with the land.

Part of anthropologist Anna Lowenhaupt Tsing's work is focused on mushrooms; for her, they gesture to how life may be lived beyond capitalism. In one of her articles, she describes how some people's lives are changed after becoming deeply involved with mushrooms:

> For Andy Moore, the wild mushroom economy, in its open opportunity for eccentrics, also creates the possibilities of vernacular science, that is, knowledge production in which ordinary people can participate. For Dr. Yoshimura, citizens' interest in environmental remediation offers the chance to build connections between human and nonhuman wellbeing. For him, efforts to re-sculpt forest landscapes make the volunteers happier and healthier even as they make a more hospitable multispecies environment.[26]

Many of the mushroom-lovers Tsing describes, enthusiasts who now devote their lives to these fungi, initially knew nothing about them or their diversity. In the same ways that mushrooms have set people onto a path of relationship with the natural world, these gestures also want to open ways for us to begin a journey from having no relationship at all with a bioregion to falling in love with the patch of land where we live. We start by walking, paying attention, slowly growing familiar with and getting closer to the beings/species around us. This process and these ritual gestures are portals that allow us to take a step toward connection: approaching, listening, touching, tasting if possible, smelling, seeing, placing skin against bark or exoskeleton or fur or flower, all the embodied means of connecting. We don't need to ask permission to start this process; everyone can learn how to bring connection into our own lives. Before we even know it, we've fallen in love with different species, and then as a matter of course with the whole environment that surrounds them.

This ritual is about bringing together simple gestures with our feelings, our intimate relationship with a bioregion, science, and the well-being of a place and all its species. These gestures act as ways of listening to the pace and laws of the land, which shift and change with any number of entanglements. Before we continue, it is important to define what I understand as the law of the land in this book.

I use this term *law of the land* as coined by Aboriginal thinker Tyson Yunkaporta's work, especially in his book *Sand Talk*,[27] where he claims that indigenous Aboriginal knowledge carries an old law, which is also called the law of the land. This law carries patterns of living, thinking, being, and doing that are rooted in relationship with the land, place, and ecosystems. It is place-based wisdom, held and passed on by elders who are the keepers of the knowledge of the land. The law of the land organizes social, spiritual, political, and economic systems in alignment with the specific landscape and elements of a place, which we are calling here bioregion. The law of the land is not the law of physics or the predetermined divine law that became the "natural law" in seventeenth-century Europe, where a certain understanding of Nature ended up regulating what was natural and what was unnatural. I am not advocating a naturalism where we have to discover these laws and follow them. Neither am I looking to the Law of God previously inscribed in nature. The law of the land here instead opens patterns and movements of the land in each bioregion that are all part of co-evolutionary processes that remain open to the relations and entanglements of beings (humans, more than humans, spirit/Spirit/s etc.) and their actions and ways of living in that place. Against the understanding of the law of nature that is fixed and never situated but universalized—that is, able to be discovered in Central Pennsylvania; the Mooca neighborhood where I was born in Sao Paulo, Brazil; or Manila, the capital of the Philippines—the law of the land as understood here is local, place-based, and emerges from the movements of the land itself. It is not something imposed but in flux and movement all the time.

Thus, when social life, governance, ecosystems, communities, religious systems, and so on are in sync with the land, it is easier to feel and see and listen to and follow the law of the land, its flows and movements. That is when a bioregion becomes an oikos, our household. However, when the laws of the land are understood as separated, imposed, disturbed or violated, we must work to reorient ourselves to the land's needs and demands so that the land itself can then reorient us again. Through these ritual practices, we can then create embassies[28] with other species, always learning how to live with, learn about, respect, and communicate with the many worlds and languages among which we exist. With time, we can learn how to work alongside the guardians of a particular place and listen to the spirits of that bioregion. The gestures I describe are intended to start us down that path—and as we learn along the journey, we will surely discover other rituals that can flourish and enhance this relationship.

Every gesture can heal us back into the land, clearing our minds, calming our thoughts, filling our hearts, tending our wounds. We know, though, that there is no purely self-achieved healing, but every healing is dependent on a larger collective of agents, be it humans, plants, animals, spirits, in various compositions, rituals and forms. And so this ritual, especially when done as a collective whose members show up with and for each other, can also be used to respond to our loneliness, allowing us to feel the earth as companion and reminding us that we are always in a relationship with something, somebody. More than that: the gestures can serve as practices of reconciliation and peace, ways that lead to conciliatory actions directed toward oneself, a group, even the land. This ritual practice brings forth the value inherent in what we thought had no value, in precious forms of life we believed were of little consequence until used for purposes of development. It demonstrates the need to care for every entity in a bioregion, to attend to the health and flourishing of all life that moves and flows within it.

But it is important to emphasize that every practice engenders a circular movement of action and response, offer and demand, givenness and obligation. Every act or gesture must involve reciprocity. As we start to relate to the land in which we live, we become responsible for that very land. The call from the earth mentioned above brings both gifts and obligations along with it; we can't just practice our ritual gestures and move on. Every gesture binds us to the beings we honor. For example, when we bow and express our gratitude to all living beings, we bind ourselves to those who have died and have made it possible for us to live. When we say thank you, we know we are here because of the way all of the beings that surround us have come together; we connect ourselves to this particular portion of land, and that means we are responsible for all the beings that dwell within it. In Portuguese, when we say *obrigado,* thank you, to someone, we are both thanking the person and binding ourselves to them. As Isabelle Stengers says,

> [I]t is clear that requirement and obligation describe a kind of topology. We require something from something or someone. We are obligated by, or are obligated to—with, in some cases—the dimension of gratitude that the Portuguese language emphasizes. The topology described distinguishes an "outside" and an "inside."[29]

To live together in that topos, in that place together, is to listen attentively to other species. Not simply to react or respond to them, but to allow ourselves to be transformed by them: a constant collective metamorphosis, a collective becoming! The animals come together with the plants and humans to continue their shared lives. The plants adjust to climate change in order to survive, and we, too must adapt along with the beings in our bioregion so that all of us may continue to live and thrive as neighbors in that particular place.

I realized when I began teaching this ritual to my students that I had only asked them to go through the gestures individually. But then I started hearing that although they were enthusiastic about the practice, they felt the need to do the ritual within a community. Now we do the gestures together, starting every class with them. And carrying them out in community has changed the practices themselves. After class, students take these new rituals to their own community, using them however they feel is needed. There is no rule about or limitation to how these gestures can be used or altered; each community and each patch of land should decide what to take, what to expand, what to leave out. It is within the collection of practices that a new spirit will emerge to move and sustain us and enhance our lives.

We need a different spirit to guide our lives, one that will help us, as it moves from and within our particular landscapes, to discover and reclaim our bioregions. This book is an invitation to get in touch with, relate to, and be oriented by *another spirit*, namely, the spirit(s) of the land that still sweeps over the face of our rivers and lakes and oceans; that dwells in the trees and the flight and song of birds; the same avian spirit that visited Jesus at his baptism. The spirit of the land can guide us in reorienting ourselves and living as much as possible in harmony with the earth. The spirit of the land directs our eyes to the plants, our ears to the birds, our hands to the soil, our hearts to the ways of care and reciprocity, and our bodies to the bodies of other beings.

In this way, we find what Donna Haraway calls a "situated knowledge,"[30] right in our own bioregion where we discover we can and must become kin with other beings, become "companion species."[31] Right there, in our environment, we are called to conjoin our lives with other species as equals, ensuring that every species has a habitat to live in and avoiding thinking and living as if only humans were allowed to occupy all spaces.

Moreover, instead of trusting in individual efforts to "get somewhere" by pulling ourselves up by our bootstraps, we might need to "invest" time in space, placing our bodies solidly within our communal existence, gardening together, working alongside each other to clean up our rivers, pressing governments to enact and enforce better laws, stopping companies that are destroying the environment, creating new ways of sourcing and using energy, responding to economic inequality, opposing environmental racism, and so much more. When we understand that everything is interconnected, we can come to a place where instead of longing for individual attention or accomplishments, we find our joy in communal forms of care and attention, forms of living that counteract the capitalist spirit of taking as much for ourselves as we can. These are the attitudes, the actions, the real-world outcomes, this book hopes to foster.

In the end, this book is an attempt at experimenting with thinking-feeling-doing something differently than the ways so many of our habits and customs have instructed us, have led us in the process into a place of destruction, a place that some call the Anthropocene. Rituals are ways of experimenting with new forms of life through thinking-feeling-doing with the land, the bioregion we live in. Every page maintains the belief that rituals can be powerful ways to help us start living otherwise. This belief is based upon the ways many Indigenous People organize their entire lives through ceremony, where all life, the entire community of beings, is present: bodies, territories, and worlds. Their thinking-feeling-doing emerges from the land and offers wisdom and complex ways of thinking. Whereas Western knowledge is complicated, Indigenous Knowledges are complex—and our time calls for more complex ways of thinking-feeling-doing. Mirroring Indigenous Knowledges, this book wants to experiment with new forms of ritual understanding about bodies, territories, and worlds: all species and systems, including human, mineral, animal, vegetable, riparian, . . . the entire earth. In this way, rituals fit in with Brazilian literary theorist Alexandre Nodari's assertion about the current role of literature, anthropology, and Indigenous Knowledges:

> I believe that the Anthropocene challenges us to experiment: to try new ways of living, of thinking, to be aware of the fallibility of these experiments, to vary them, to open ourselves to variation, since the modern experience, which claims to be universal, is leading our world to destruction, dragging with it so many other worlds and their experiences, which have much to teach us.[32]

CHAPTER FOUR

The spirit/Spirit/s in the Bioregion

It can be strange to talk about "spirit/Spirit/s" today, because the concept is both hard to pin down and used to support all manner of generalized assumptions. But since the crisis of our time is a spiritual one, we need to reinstate this notion and all the worlds it can engender. For our purposes, we are speaking about the spirit of the land. There is a fundamental correlation, formation, and mutual belonging between spirit/Spirit/s and beings, human, more-than-human, and the land. In that way, there is a cosmological orientation of the spirit/Spirit/s to our living. In its this-worldly dimension, it takes the form of what some Indigenous Peoples call the Great Spirit of Mother Earth[33]—a spirit that can only be perceived within a specific bioregion. For example, the Buddhist scholar Aiping Cao is able to devise rainmaking rituals for her particular part of the world, thanks to her knowledge of Buddhist history within and beyond China *and* the presence of her region's dragon spirit: *both* are required in order for the ritual to be effective. Cao cannot perform the same ritual anywhere else in the world, since it is dependent upon the action of that particular land's spirit; it is *that spirit* that brings the rain.

The notion of the spirit/Spirit/s—that force in Jewish traditions called ruach, in Christianity the Holy Spirit, and in some Indigenous communities the Great Spirit—also points to the existence of a fundamental inhabiting presence whose full immanence is possible only in relation with all beings in a given place: animals, plants, humans, and so on. Some other people will call spirit or spirits or a combination of both. The spirit/Spirit/s is a vital force that suffuses our experiences, connects with our senses, and orients our personal and collective forms of life. The spirit/Spirit/s here is an energy that has the power to maintain and destroy the balance of our entire existence.

For that balance to be achieved and maintained, we—all the beings within a place—must work together.

Growing up as a Christian, I learned that the Holy Spirit was free and could not be controlled: "The wind blows where it chooses, and you hear the sound of it, but you do not know where it comes from or where it goes."[34] The notion of the Holy Spirit was understood, among other things, as something opposed to the flesh, the human body. To be spiritual was to live in the Spirit and in denial of the flesh and its dangerous desires and erratic ways. Second, the Holy Spirit was considered to be a presence not to be confused with any person, space, thing, or action. Here, any association of the Spirit with any particular object or creature was idolatry; if specifically related to the land, that spirit was a pagan notion—no longer a part of Christianity. Third, the Holy Spirit's deepest connection was to time and history. This spirit was attached to a Hegelian telos, a movement toward the fullness of a given time.

Christianity for the most part has turned the Holy Spirit into a presence of the inner self of the believer, a feeling in the heart, a voice in our head. Withdrawing its own presence from the land, the Holy Spirit started to live mostly in the subjectivity of the Christian believer and was only named in some exterior events where the theological rational interpretation would fit the event at stake. The Reformation of the sixteenth century was fundamental to this process when Luther moved the presence of the Holy Spirit from the outward site of the Eucharistic Host to the feeling within the heart of the believer. When reading the epistle of Romans, the work of the Holy Spirit defines the forms of God's revelation to the interior chambers of the mind and the heart. Luther comments on his own inner transformation reading Paul's Letter to the Romans:

> Now I felt as though I had been reborn altogether and had entered Paradise. In the same moment the face of the whole of Scripture became apparent to me. My mind ran through the Scriptures, as far as I was able to recollect them, seeking analogies in other phrases, such as the works of God, by which he makes us strong, the wisdom of God, by which he makes us wise, the strength of God, the salvation of God, the glory of God. Through this word the Holy Spirit enlightened me in the tower.[35]

Modernity has also turned all knowledge from place-based knowledge to interior knowing. It turned all of the spirit/Spirit/s of the land into an interiority, disconnecting us from the land. The enlightenment was something to be found within, searching for the courage within to free oneself. Moreover, to know that we exist comes from thinking and doubting. The interiorization of knowledge and the subjectification of the spirit/Spirit/s emptied the presence of the spirit/Spirit/s from the land, the exterior immanent world we lived to the inner world we are now destined to solely deal with forever. Bruno Latour, in his book *An Inquiry into Modes of Existence. An Anthropology of the Moderns*, says that we moderns live in the mode of metamorphosis, that he defines as mutations, emotions, influences, divinities, that "explores the differences."[36] Anthropologist Eduardo Viveiros de Castro, following Bruno Latour and citing indigenous Xaman Davi Kopenawa, defines what we have done with the notion of the spirit, that I am calling the spirit/Spirit/s:

> While non modern people tend to give to this mode a much more ontological consideration, moderns tend to confine this mode of metamorphosis to the interiority of the psyche, that is, we tend to reduce this entire mode to subjectivity. The spirits (in the plural) become the spirit, something like the notion of *mind* in French... From the moment this mode of metamorphosis begins to be internalized in the psyche, the result of this is what Kopenawa said: "White people sleep a lot but only dream about themselves." That is, a huge portion of the exterior has become interior, and the world has fallen silent. The voices are now only in our heads.[37]

It was only thanks to Christian theologians such as Nancy Cardoso, Ivone Gebara, Pedro Casaldáliga, Leonardo Boff, and Vitor Westhelle and others that I learned that the markers of the Spirit were also, and fundamentally, found within a particular place. And in time, I was able to understand, via a combination of science, Buddhism, philosophy, anthropology, and fundamentally Indigenous Knowledges, that space and time go together, that time without space is transcendence—but time along with space is immanence, presence in fullness.

In this book, then, spirit/Spirit/s is understood to be a living presence connected to the land and a certain bioregion. Similar and yet very different from the Western philosophical religious tradition. When Descartes thought about reason; Augustine, Luther, or Calvin thought about God, their ideas were very local but took on universal assumptions and traveled around the world. In a similar fashion, the Spirit of capitalism has become a universal Spirit. The way to break its power is to be fully present within our own bioregions and learn about the spirit/Spirit/s as manifested from within and by the confluence of nature and culture that occurs in that patch of the world where we live. We need, according to social scientist Emmanuele Coccia, "a phenomenology of the spirit beyond the human: it must assume, albeit implicitly, that life thinks and speaks everywhere."[38] Hopefully, with many voices everywhere, we can learn to dream about other beings and not only about ourselves.

This book is precisely about the search for life that thinks and speaks everywhere. To take part in that search, we need to turn our ears to the land, we need to learn the languages of other beings, learn with the spirit/Spirit/s of the place and regain a deeper awareness that we are deeply entangled with the land on which we stand. In this process, we must do our best to avoid romanticizing the land. The aim isn't mere conservation; it isn't an attempt to uncover a proper understanding of nature as wilderness, or somehow to live tidily within entangled relations. We have lost our ability to listen to the land, we have caused too much damage to the earth; we have extinguished too much of the life about which we speak; the conditions we live in are poisonous, rough and very frail. As we begin to connect with the land through the gestures, we must learn the multiform, complex relationships already in place, as they are and see in what ways we can enter these processes and possibly help. It is not difficult: when we look for life in the places we inhabit, we are searching for that which makes us who we are. There, where we are, with whom we belong, we must learn how to interpret the clues offered by the place and the beings who live there and to move in a way that reduces death and sustains what should be kept alive. The three gestures offered in this book are but a beginning into an ontological turn in our lives, that is, to see life everywhere we look.

By engaging in these spiritual practices as more conscious ways of relating to the land, we begin by acknowledging how the spirit of capitalism has conditioned us. When we think about capitalism, we are not just thinking about an economic structure that exists apart from politics or ecology; nor do we view the economy as a form of deterministic fate, the planet's sole driving force that functions in isolation from everything else. When we talk about capitalism we are thinking about a social, familial, geographical, cultural, educational, ecological, bodily, spiritual (...) metastasized structure that shapes our lives. Capitalism is a system that has infused its spirit within us all and within our lifeways to such a degree that it has severed our ability to see life's interdependencies and understand that all aspects of life are related to and correlated with each other.

The three gestures' fundamental intention is to help us regain, consciously and unconsciously, an awareness of these relations, help us cast away the spirit of capitalism and then be possessed by the spirit/Spirit/s of the land. The intentionality invoked here aims to help us reignite deeper connections with the worlds around us; recognize that every species and life-form, from insects, plants, trees, birds, opossums, to water and more, is fundamental to our very survival since they are a part of us. Without them, we can't live! The intention then, is to establish a relationship with other beings in our immediate vicinity, to animate the powers that are present in the places we call home, and hopefully to create in the ritual practitioner a demand to live in reciprocity with those beings.

The gestures offered here do help me pay attention to other beings around me, to the functioning and thriving of their own communities, to the ways their presence demands I reorient my own habits and customs. For example, if I pay attention to the opossums, the deer, the foxes, the squirrels, the rivers, the plants, and the birds where I live, I cannot allow one more green space to be destroyed so that yet another condominium will go up for the sake of human buildings and destroy the home of all these beings. I cannot allow roads to be laid down anywhere I want. When we design and construct a neighborhood, we are responsible for finding ways of providing space, shelter, home, and food for all species living in that area.

The intention driving this ritual aims at creating the conditions that allow for reciprocal relations to emerge between the animate powers: between me and the other beings around me. Engaging in this ritual is meant to connect beings; when that happens, we grow to an awareness of others and begin the process of mutual care. That is when the molecular revolution starts.[39] The space between the gestures' intention and the molecular revolution is filled with the encounter of animate powers who together produce an efficacious transformation.

That encounter looks something like this: There is a tree on the street where I live; I've never paid attention to it before. But when I begin rising, bowing, and touching the ground beneath that tree, I start to pay closer attention to it. But attention is something that arises between beings; instead of my capturing anything, I am attuned to and by the tree.[40] This related attunement between the two of us creates a mutual belonging that then makes me care for the tree, since the tree is already caring for me. By starting to pay attention to that tree, I also start to pay attention to other beings who depend on it, as well as to the other trees in that area, and on and on. Then I begin to recognize the biodiversity around me, a diversity that can only survive if I care for all the creatures who contribute to it. The gestures' intentionality creates a form of responsibility and mutuality that will lead me to think about how to protect this tree and all the other beings around us. Thus, the result of these intentional gestures is an unmistakable entanglement between animate powers—me, the tree, and other beings—that produces in me a responsibility to care for these beings and for the entire place I live in. That nascent responsibility has set the molecular revolution in motion, the revolution that gets underway when I along with other people organize around these beings, and come together within a neighborhood or small community to care for them, fight together for the enactment and enforcement of policies that preempt their destruction, and maintain means of protecting us all.

We also work from the assumption that every being has a guiding spirit that is responsible for them. Thus, the space between my intentionality and the ensuing molecular revolution is located in the movement of the spirit/Spirit/s of the land within me and the beings around me as we reconnect. These spirit/Spirit/s are able to exorcise the spirit of capitalism, which is marked by carelessness for other beings and lack of attention to natural worlds. With the intentionality of these gestures, we become water warriors, forest warriors, river warriors, plant warriors, bird warriors, tree warriors, opossum warriors, bioregion warriors, and so on.

Even though I would not call us shamans or magicians, there is a magic that happens in these encounters; there is a certain movement of the spirit/Spirit/s in those solicitations, a new spirituality. That movement reflects something of what David Abram, US ecologist and philosopher, says of the shaman and his/her/their magic, their

> ability to readily slip out of the perceptual boundaries that demarcate his or her particular culture—boundaries reinforced by social customs, taboos, and most importantly, the common speech or language—in order to make contact with, and learn from, the other powers in the land. His magic is precisely this heightened receptivity to the meaningful solicitations—songs, cries, gestures—of the larger, more-than-human field.[41]

In these interactions, we enfold ourselves into each other, beyond sociocultural limits, free from defined concepts or proper language. We learn as we go, belonging unequivocally to each other. These connecting events, these *meaningful solicitations*, entail what Maurice Merleau-Ponty calls the passage of nature: "the passage of nature corresponds to the unity of the perceiving body and therefore to the body itself as an event and constitutes the unity of the body with other observers and with a nature for many."[42] These perceptual relationships between bodies and the places we live constitute nature; in the process, they avoid making a distinction or opposition between humans and culture.

Our task then is to create embassies between all living creatures, learning each other's voices and considering them essential to any human political, cultural, or economic decision. As we engage with a multiplicity of life-forms and intelligences, our intuition expands, our senses are amplified, and in that unique moment, we experience a relationship with some-body, for every form of life has a body. We become who we are and have always been: "nature." In the worlds of Merleau-Ponty, "we are the parents of a Nature of whom we are the children."[43]

All of these connections between humans and more-than-humans constitute the phenomenology of the "spirit beyond the human," as Coccia calls it. With these three gestures, *meaningful solicitations* take place, and the entire earth will become what we already are, namely: animated. Ancestral connections will start to reappear; we will begin to speak in the many languages of plants, fireflies, waters, agouti, birds, coral reefs, and octopuses. The supersensuous life will grow; the immanent-transcendent will show itself in all its presence and otherness as the unexpected starts to unfold and that which was previously unconsidered is seen in full. We will fly through the skies with the eagles, feel the majestic maturity of the rocks; we will climb the mountains with the bighorn, rise from the earth with the corn and the rice, go underground with the roots; we will flow with the rivers, burn with the fire, dream with the stones, make honey with the bees, and roar with the jaguar.

In that way, the spirit/Spirit/s as understood here live in and through configurations of humans and all other beings, so that it is alive in a tree, a land, a river, an animal, a human. Each being possesses various forms of knowledge, emotion, relation, and revelation. David Abram says:

> While the notion of "spirit" has come to have, for us in the West, a primarily anthropomorphic or human association, my encounter with the ants was the first of many experiences suggesting to me that the "spirits" of an indigenous culture are primarily those modes of intelligence or awareness that do not possess a human form... Moreover, it is not only those entities acknowledged by Western civilization as "alive," not only the other animals and the plants that speak, as spirits, to the senses of an oral culture, but also the meandering river from which those animals drink, and the torrential monsoon rains, and the stone that fits neatly into the palm of the hand. The mountain, too, has its thoughts. The forest birds whirring and chattering as the sun slips below the horizon are vocal organs of the rain forest itself.[44]

Davi Kopenawa, Yanomami Xaman from the Amazon, carries in his people's ways of living (his ontology), exactly that sort of larger phenomenology of the bioregion's spirit/Spirit/s:

> What we call Urihinari are the spirits of the forest: the spirits of the trees huutihiri pë, the spirits of the leaves yaahanari pë and the spirits of the vines thoothoxiri pë. These spirits are very numerous and play on the forest floor. We call them urihi a, "nature," as do the animal spirits yarori pë and even those of bees, turtles or snails. The "fertility value" of the forest, which we call në rope a, is also "nature" for us: it was created with the forest, it is its "wealth." The forest earth has a vital breath, wixia, which is very long. That of human beings is short: we live and die quickly. If we do not deforest it, the forest does not die. It does not decompose. It is thanks to its moist breath that plants grow. When we are very sick, in a ghost state, this breath also helps us to heal. So we borrowed it and we were fine... This breath comes from deep in the forest floor, from where its freshness lives. It also lives in its waters.[45]

It is within each bioregion that the spirit/Spirit/s will take on a unique form, a sound, a name, a different understanding, relation, and perspective. The spirit/Spirit/s can be the energy/essence/nature/modes of a being, a rock, a manufactured thing. The spirit/Spirit/s of the land can be connected with the spirit that lives in us humans through our minds, bodies, and spirits. We might say that an era's zeitgeist is the Spirit of a collective mindset, of the moral climate of the time in which one lives—but only if this Spirit is not the sole domain or possession of human actions or presence, but is instead the spirit/Spirit/s of a bioregional collective, a spirit/Spirit/s that relates to all beings living in that place.

The Amazonian Tukano People also have a unique relationship to the guardians of the land, which are called Waimahsã. Tukano scholar João Paulo Lima Barreto describes the Waimahsã:

> The Waimahsã are creatures that possess the same qualities and capabilities as humans, including their physical appearance, but are invisible to ordinary people in everyday life. They can only be seen by a specialist, Yai or Kumu, or in dreams—situations that even allow for interaction between them. They are responsible for, guardians of, or protectors of the spaces and all the animals that roam within them, which does not, however, make them "owners" of these animals, but rather of the spaces themselves. The Waimahsã are also beings of multiple natures, as they are capable of developing qualities and abilities of animals and plants to act in certain situations. Given their complexity, finding a translation that encompasses it is a task I chose to forgo in this work.

The Tukano believe it is essential to know how to live with the Waimahsã and establish good relationships with them. Barreto says:

> Another important issue is maintaining good relations with the Waimahsã. To achieve this, humans must adopt certain behaviors and follow some basic etiquette or good manners. As mentioned previously, land space, water space, forest space, and air space are the homes of the Waimahsã. Therefore, to use or even move through these spaces, humans must ask their permission.

For Indigenous people living in South America, each unique place has its own particular subjects (animals, birds, fish, plants, forests), knowledge, and forms of relationship. For each bioregion there is a specific story, myth, symbol, song, dance, cosmology, and spirit/Spirit/s.

Those of us guided by the assumptions of modernity, though, tend not to consider any of these things. Used as we are to approaching our neighborhoods according to a nature/culture divide, we see them as places inhabited only by human beings. When we move to a neighborhood, we tend to think of the area in terms of the class, race, and ethnicity of the people who live there. We fail to consider the larger landscape, the bioregion with its waters and plants, its birds and fish. For example, when my daughter and I took tours of college campuses, we were introduced to every building without hearing any mention of the many trees or birds surrounding them. And even if we do consider a place's more-than-human presences, it is not as real subjects. Our world is mostly made up of human beings.

For Indigenous communities in the Amazon, however, every space is filled with subjects. Anthropologist Eduardo Viveiros de Castro says that

> This eminently social aspect of the relationship between society and nature is at the origin of Amerindian cosmological reflection. It contrasts markedly with the conception of nature projected by Western modernity. If we could characterize in a few words a basic attitude of indigenous cultures, we would say that the relationships between a society and the components of its environment are conceived and experienced as social relationships, that is, relationships between people.[46]

The fish is a central figure in the life of the Tukano. Although Waimahsã means fish-people, when Barreto asks his father whether the fish are people, he doesn't receive a straight answer. His father, he says, "stops, thinks, and turns to the kihti of origin of the world and the statements of the practice of bahsesse." The presence and meaning and cosmology of the fish are variable and complex. In that sense, the subjectivity of the fish depends on the knowledge of the people and the fish's context in a given situation.

Understanding how Indigenous peoples relate to place through cosmological frameworks—seeing fish as people, recognizing every space as filled with subjects—helps us see what we've lost under capitalism's zeitgeist. To reclaim this relational way of being, we need to understand what I mean by spirit/Spirit/s in this book and how it differs from the narrow, human-centered "spirit of the times" that capitalism offers us.

As we currently understand the concept, the zeitgeist is a capitalist presence that takes into consideration only a small portion—not even the whole—of the human population. In order for the zeitgeist to be a certain era's Spirit of time and place, it must consider the spirits of the animals, the trees, the rivers, the mountains, and so on. To allow the spirit/Spirit/s of the land to reorient the ways we live, we must undergo constant metamorphosis, since our relationships with and connections to the place will demand we change.[47] As we enter into a deeper connection with the land, we will have to create embassies of connection as we learn how to "speak" with beings to whom we have not paid enough attention. To establish a connection means we learn their ways of living. Then, as we make alliances with other beings, whether animals, plants, trees, mountains, rivers, bees, birds, and so on, and grow into a deeper familiarity with the living beings in that place and the Spirit/s that is/are related to them, the ontologies that feed our modes of existence on the planet will continue to change. Thus, the ways we relate to each being in each particular place will order our lives according to forms of mutual belonging, and the spirit/Spirit/s of the land will infuse our unfolding cosmologies with rich ontological presence.

In this book, spirit/Spirit/s refers to the web of subjectivities found throughout the earth, since the earth mothers all forms of being. In giving life and being to everything that is, earth creates, guides, and orients relationships and forms of connectivity among all beings, organizing life in myriad ways. We could say that the idea of the Spirit is interwoven with the deep and complex relationships between home, land, and heart. As environmental activist and poet Gary Snyder says, "The heart of a place is the home, and the heart of the home is the fire pit, the hearth."[48] The hearth is the unique location on earth where ideas and experiences are first lived; the hearth then travels with us, taking shape wherever we tell stories with the other beings found there; the hearth is found within the songlines we attach to placetimes. It encompasses not only landscapes and soundscapes, but also singing-scapes, touching-scapes, tasting- and smelling- and feeling-scapes, intuition- and mind-scapes, and so on.

It is in these places that the spirit/Spirit/s live and move and orient the beings found within them, the multiplicity of spirits all contained within Gaia, which animates the world. Humans, though, shape and are shaped by the spirit/Spirit/s of the earth according to the *law* of the land and the *lore* of the land. That is, our existence is in large measure determined by the life-forms unique to our bioregion; it is conditioned by the stories we learn from the earth and from each other, by the ways we talk about the Spirits we see, hear, feel, learn, understand, and receive. The spirit/Spirit/s flows through and is found within the living earth, "the great nourishing subjectivity—at once both Spiritual and material—that sustains all that is."[49] Moreover, every patch of land will have its own forms of living, of its fabulations, and of its entanglements. Each bioregion, which is already a region of another region, will have its forms of organization made by its own living organisms, with its own subjectivities, having its own species caring for other species, its own custodians taking care of other forms of life. The natural and the supernatural are both distinct and blurred in each place. As Brazilian writer Clarice Lispector says: "The natural is also supernatural. Don't think it's far away. The natural itself is a mystery."[50]

Thus, when we talk in this book about a *spiritual* practice, we are talking about a way of immersing ourselves deeply within the places where we live, the natural/supernatural environment of which we are a part, and to which we contribute, each of us fully inhabiting that particular region, our bioregion. When we are fully alive within our own bioregions, we are also fully open to spiritual practices. As Japanese Zen Buddhist monk Dōgen once said, "When you find your place where you are, practice occurs."[51]

How much of your neighborhood do you really know? Not long ago I visited my mother, who still lives in the same place I grew up. It was only then, after fifty years, that I realized I didn't know anything about my neighborhood other than the people who lived there. I started to pay attention to the trees I had grown up with; I had never really noticed them before. A walk around my neighborhood revealed that there were almost thirty kinds of trees living in an area of only a few blocks.[52] It was the fullness of the trees' presence in me, around my home, heart, and land that caused me to recognize myself as a spiritual being; it was the excess of presence flowing from the flora and fauna that caused me to recognize it all as part of my once-alienated being. That is the re(li)gion of my life!

We have two ways of being spiritual: one is to be captivated by the spirit of capitalism that has taken over every single institution of our societies: religions, schools, financial organizations, sports clubs, places of leisure, government departments and offices, and more. The other way of being spiritual is to have our re(li)gion imbued with the thousands of earth-presences within us as we live some-where. I would go as far as saying that there is no spirit in us other than the capitalist one if we walk around without seeing, listening, and paying attention to the plants, the trees, the animals, the rivers.

I remember my mother visiting me in the United States; we would go out for a walk, even though she was in her eighties and we had to move slowly. In that walk, we would stop at every flower and plant along the way. My mother would check on their health; she would touch some of them, comparing them to the ones she knew in Brazil. But she would give all of them unique greetings: "How beautiful you are!" or "Oh you are not looking good, I hope you get better." That walk was a powerful spiritual walk, precisely because it was not an isolated walk-in-itself, but one that involved other presences that provided my mother with an excess of presence, a presence that started to fill her heart with the spirit/Spirit/s of that particular patch of land. In the attention that was paid to all beings we encountered, that walk was a way to cast out the demon of capitalism.

All of the beings of a place, its fauna, flora, bodies of water and so on, will not make me "spiritual" just by their presence. People can work in their gardens without feeling any sense of spirituality. The turning point lies in the growing awareness that all these places are filled with beings who are fully alive, pulsing and sensing the world in some very specific ways and that There is/are spirit/Spirit/s who owns them, relate to them, care for them, and protect them. The more I see the earth as alive, and all its beings as fully alive, "with Spirit within,"[53] not as a mirror to myself but whole other worlds of differences surrounding me, the less I will be able or willing to view them not as inanimate beings for me to use or explore as resources—but will instead recognize them as beings I must respect and honor, and do so with respect and a full sense that I need to learn so I can perhaps start a relationship. When I start to see myself as one living being among many, maybe thousands or millions, my spirituality begins to fully flourish.

It is only when these beings become part of our conscious living that we become spiritual. Thus, each of us needs to be deeply familiar with our particular bioregion, able not only to recognize the life it contains but also to understand how each individual life makes a home for itself, and in doing so, contributes to the lives of other beings. For example, every day in the Amazon, the agoutis move through the forest eating some seeds and storing others to eat later, hiding their day's harvest in buried caches. In the process, some buried seeds are forgotten and left behind, not only helping trees to survive as the seeds continue to reforest the area, but also producing additional seeds that the agoutis will be able to eat in the future.

Fascinating! That is spiritual work, work that depends on the full presence of others. It is the opposite of capitalism, where the desire is for the other's erasure so that I may have more for myself.

We must be closely acquainted, then, with our region's climate; with its rivers, plants, animals, and birds; with the ways these beings survive and thrive so that we can enter into this spiritual flow of full mutual life. When we do that, we also realize that there is not only emergent and flourishing life around us, but threats and emergencies announced by each species that demand we listen and help.[54] If we are able to see these multiple planes of existence, the many species-worlds and their unique relationship with the laws of the land, we will ultimately understand the land's law and its lore, the spirit/Spirit/s of the land. In doing that, and learning about the lore of the place's longtime inhabitants, we might discover that there was, has been, or might be a spirit that still lives there, one that owns a tree, or honors a river, or is telling us how to establish balance within the biore(li)gion.

Thus, it is our task to listen to the spirit/Spirit/s of the earth in each patch of land, in each bioregion, and figure out how to live in that place. In order to do that, we need to take an inventory of the places we inhabit so that we can learn with those we had never paid attention to but who have always lived there, with us. For instance, when I am in New York, I need to know the Hudson River as much as the parks around me; I need to know Harlem, the people on the streets, the gardens and the types of trees that grow there. I have to learn with animals, like the pigeons and the rats, who have figured out how to live in this jungle of cement; I need to understand how they survive and know how to ensure that no species (human or other) overwhelms any given place. Taking this inventory is a spiritual practice!

The ritual practice offered here aims to help us see and cherish every being that lives in my neighborhood, every aspect of that being's life, even if it's hard to see. It must operate according to "the way," David Abram observed, that "the senses themselves have, of throwing themselves beyond what is immediately given, in order to make tentative contact with the other sides of things that we do not sense directly, with the hidden or invisible aspects of the sensible."[55] It is only from and within my neighborhoods in New York and central Pennsylvania, and all of the beings there with me, that my spiritual thinking and feeling flourish and can become universal.

FIGURE 2 *A cup of death.*

CHAPTER FIVE

Global Spirit and Local spirit/Spirit/s

As we pay attention to the local, we realize that there is a global spirit in capitalism that tends to define our own neighborhoods. To understand how we live within our neighborhoods, we have to attend to political scientist Nancy Fraser's assertion that megacorporations "are basically sucking dry the wealth, health, energies and capacities of working people all over the globe. So, we, the working people, are being cannibalized by the capitalist class."[56] This process isn't hard to see. The Coke we drink comes thanks to the privatization of water sources in someone else's neighborhood; the gold in our jewelry thanks to Indigenous lands seized by mining companies. Large fishing conglomerates steal small villages' sources of sustenance, and oil companies drill into the grounds of people and more than humans habitats, ripping apart their very households.

While we must learn and confront the financial capitalist movements bearing down upon all of us, we must act locally. There is where our molecular revolutions can happen! As we strengthen our connection to the land on which we live, the less we will become able to agree to the presence and practices of national or global conglomerates draining the wealth from our neighborhoods. It may be too much to ask, too large a task to imagine—but we must connect our own small worlds to those of others, together finding the spirit/Spirit/s of the land for our shared struggle. Indigenous Brazilians teach us where to look for what will bring us together; as they say, "The land is the mother of all struggles."

CHAPTER SIX

Discernment of the spirit/Spirit/s

However, there is no simple or single story of capitalism, nor is there a single duality between the spirit of capitalism and the spirit/Spirit/s of the land. A multiplicity of patterns and processes is happening all the time and everywhere. The movements of the spirit of capitalism and the spirit/Spirit/s of the land will always involve confusion, blurring, complexity, and crooked paths, clarity and lack of it. We will recognize, understand, and know what to do in some places, conditions, structures, and movements; other situations will be unfamiliar, and will require close study.

In today's so-called marketplace of ideas, a plethora of individualistic spiritualities compete for people's attention, churning out promises of change via a few particular steps.

The market of spiritualities creates and addresses itself to nearly infinite, conflicting modes of attention. This ubiquitous demand for our attention confuses our desires and our habits of consumption. But the gestures I describe are neither individualistic nor uncompromised, and instead of tempting us with created desires, help us to access our own legitimate ones. A means of committing and assuming responsibility for all creatures, this ritual does not promise personal happiness, but the happiness of an entire bioregion. It takes a lifetime's worth of work and dedication, carried out with consistency and flexibility, carried out with others, just to scratch the surface of what needs doing. And so it is important to carry out these gestures together with other people to help us discern the presence of the spirit/Spirit/s. As the book of Proverbs says, "in an abundance of counselors there is safety."[57]

As much as this text might seem to present a number of forces as being opposed to each other—different spirits, Indigenous and non-Indigenous Knowledges, individuals and communities—those forces are both unique and inextricably tied together. Non-Indigenous Knowledges are just as fundamental as Indigenous Knowledges—and Indigenous Knowledges, when not used properly, can also do harm. Movement and flow, give and take, occur across the apparent divide. For example, engaging in ritual gestures beside a river, and thus acquiring deeper knowledge of it, a hydraulic engineer and an Indigenous person can both make essential contributions to caring for that river; they are both part of the communities who live near and depend on it. We must always discern which spirit/Spirit/s are present and necessary as we go forward.

The same discernment is required where our desires and convictions are concerned. How do I distinguish between commitment to the religion of the earth and the religion of capitalism?[58] The good and the bad, the creative and the destructive? All are always present, always part of our very selves and the worlds in which we live, and there is often no clear division between one and the other. Contradictions abound.

No desire is pure; it is even hard to know what we really desire. One of Søren Kierkegaard's assumptions is that "purity of the heart is to will one thing," an assertion that refers to St. Augustine's question, "What do I love when I love my God?"[59] and to Jesus's declaration that "where your heart is, there is your treasure."[60] But who is able to will or desire just one thing? Christians have been instructed to desire God and God alone. Even if the one thing is not God, how is only one desirable thing possible in our consumer-capitalist society, where we have been taught and encouraged to stretch our desires to infinity, to chase our wants into eternity and end up desiring desire itself? Our spirituality has become this desiring of desire, and our true desires have become lost in the midst.

The ritual I describe in the book intends to channel Augustine's and Kierkegaard's abstract notions of desire into the desire for the earth. Its gestures are meant to turn our hearts toward the earth, to see the earth as our deepest treasure. Perhaps then we can understand earth's desires, as in the following Brazilian song:

> Caress the earth
> Know the earth's desires
> Earth's heat, the propitious season
> And fertilize the soil[61]

It is within our blurry, confusing lifestyles, our jumbled ways of desiring and knowing, that these gestures can help us gain clarity, together. Thinking and practicing this ritual on our own won't take us anywhere. But if we make these gestures together, constantly, as a form of devotion, we may be able to change some things in the short term, others in the long term; still others will be left to generations that follow. We must begin our new practices right here, right now, joining along with others for whom these practices are anything but new. If we can learn how to caress the earth, know earth's desires . . . perhaps we can learn together how to live in true relationship with the earth.

CHAPTER SEVEN

The Economy of Beatitudes and Shimmering

Something happens to us when we start to connect with the land. Our senses awaken through a certain beatitudization. A certain happiness emerges, a different kind of peace; we notice we are more grounded, perhaps less anxious, more trusting. Beatitude indicates a state of bliss; its Latin root, beātificus, comes from the verb beāre, which means "to make happy, gladden, bless."[62] All earthlings have this power of gladdening things, beings, and places. When we tend the soil we are blessed; when we listen to the birds we are glad; and when we care for plants we cause happiness to abound!

To reconnect with the land is to break centuries of disconnection. When we show up to and for the land, we feel the grace the land always has in store for us, honoring us with its presence. When we pay close attention to the land, we begin to see beatitudes—happiness, gladness, and blessings—everywhere! We start to see, as many Indigenous People tell us, that each bioregion has its own law. Not a fixed law, not a divine law written somewhere else, but a law consisting of flexible patterns that organize life, moving, shifting, and ordering it via movements both seen and unforeseen. It is these patterns that are present in a name Christians have used for the earth: the oikos of God, the household of God. That home has its own patterns, structures, ebbs and flows, its own billion forms of life. Every bioregion has its own immanent-transitory laws that are always in movement, in millions of combinations, in billions of forms of symbiosis.

Modernity declared that nature was static, but that is so far from the truth! Nature as defined here is fully alive and filled with movement. Every earthling possesses agency, a way of creating and recreating life, moving and finding new forms of living. The earth is fully alive, pulsing in many forms, according to distinct beats in different places. Nature always operates according to an ever-transforming dynamic through different living beings.

Static nature would be a dead place without agency. Surely death and life, suffering and blessings, are present throughout the earth, all part of the earth's own movement, processes that in themselves are wondrous and awe-inspiring.

When we practice these ritual gestures, then we are counteracting the human forces of death: agribusiness, extractivism, and capitalism's profit-driven destruction of every last biome. We engage in this practice to learn and enter into the dynamic flows and patterns each bioregion teaches us, which in turn reveal to us both our limits and the ways we must care for and protect the land. Although fully alive, the earth is not eternal, and can die. The earth cares for us and demands not only that we care for and act as its guardians, but also serve as agents of happiness and blessings. Our task is to protect the vitality of every earthling, to bless every place, to work for a happy life for all, fending off the many destabilizing, sadness-inducing energies that capitalism brings with it.

We could call the beatitude I have spoken about *shimmering*, which means shining with a soft, slightly wavering light. To shimmer is to be taken up by the light of the earth. The earth, though, is losing its own light, as its intricately interwoven systems, patterns, and processes are strained and break down. For example, if the little agouti in the Amazon are killed, the forest will be unable to replenish its trees. The presence of new trees depends upon the agouti hiding, and then forgetting about, the trees they have stored under the soil. The agouti are shimmering presences in the forest that allow the forest itself to take up that light and shimmer as well.

It is thanks to Australian ethnographer Deborah Bird Rose, who wrote extensively on Aboriginal Australians, that I learned to pay attention to the shimmering power of the earth. In her article "Shimmer When All You Love Is Being Trashed,"[63] she describes the deep connection between eucalyptus trees and flying foxes. The foxes are lured to the taste of the trees' flowers; when they eat them, the foxes help pollinate the trees. Rose tells us that "Both trees and flying foxes depend on these encounters. The tongue meets the flower and the flower meets the tongue in a kiss of symbiotic mutualism. Trees call out to flying foxes in languages of color and scent, and flying foxes respond with gusto."[64]

A "reciprocal capture" occurs between tree and fox that results in the creation of more life. Bees and birds also feast on the tree's flowers: life abounds. Rose defines shimmering using Isabelle Stengers's concept of reciprocal capture:

> I use the concept of shimmer to frame this chapter because I believe it is susceptible to a "reciprocal capture" with Western thought. For philosopher Isabelle Stengers, "reciprocal capture" is "an event, the production of new, immanent modes of existence" in which neither entity transcends the other or forces the other to bow down. It is a process of

> encounter and transformation, not absorption, in which different ways of being and doing find interesting things to do together.[65]

However, this deep and ancient connection is at risk of disappearing; humans are afraid of flying foxes, consider them pests, and kill them. Rose's work shows how the members of ecological communities must live together, depending on each other for survival, just as the trees depend on the flying foxes and vice versa. The food and nourishment, life and joy, growth and reproduction of these beings form an intrinsic, tight web of connection. Rose shows, though, how deeply the forces of death found in colonization and ongoing forms of genocide eat away at these relationships: the disintegration of the world we are experiencing now. Her pain at witnessing the process led to her learning from Aboriginal teachers the power of the earth's overall shimmering, which offered her a way of coping and moving forward, even as her work begin "when the worlds that one loves—including angiosperms and flying foxes—are being trashed."[66]

Thus, to live within beatitudes, Australians must cheer their patch of earth by protecting the flying foxes. They and we must awaken to the need to protect a whole plane of immanence; we must learn to see the transcendent web of life right before us. But how do we do that? The three gestures help us enter into the many ways available for us to see that web and take action. Rose defines exactly the aim of this ritual practice:

> I have been adopted into a group of flying fox people, and for me this has been an astonishingly powerful lure, calling me to consider how I might live an ethic of kinship and care within this multispecies family. With it comes a burden: the commitment to bear witness to the shimmering, lively, powerful, interactive worlds that ride the waves of ancestral power. This commitment calls me to engage in forms of scholarship that encourage "passionate immersion" in the lives of both humans and nonhumans.[67]

To shimmer is to gain the capacity of joy, a beatitude! We must search for the wonder-filled experience of shimmering: "Shimmer, or brilliance, is—people say—one's actual capacity to see and experience ancestral power. This is to say that when one is captured by shimmer, one experiences not only the joy of the visual capture but also, and more elegantly as one becomes more knowledgeable, ancestral power as it moves actively across the world."[68]

We must be de-captured by the spirit of capitalism and be captured instead by the power of shimmering! Shimmering, beatitudes, desires, spirit, and power: to be captured is to be seized by entire worlds. This is true whether those are the worlds of capitalism or of shimmering/beatitude; we must determine which worlds live in us, in our minds, hearts, and bodies. To be able to go on while the world crumbles before our eyes, we must shimmer and see the earth shimmering. This is a practice, and a constant one; once we see the shimmering of ecological communities, we become iridescent too! The brightness of the earth will illuminate our shadows; when we see and contribute to our region's beatitude, we too will find happiness.

Beatitudes and shimmering are part of the stories of loving ecological communities whose members serve each other, enticing each other with delicious gifts, offering their shimmering so that future generations will also gain their own shimmering. Shimmering is about mutual gifts and influences, about the interconnectedness among species, we humans and all other species in a disintegrating world. Those interconnections are the very shimmering of life that pulses everywhere in the midst of destruction, violence, brutality, and death. To shimmer is to keep oneself alive! To make the world happy is to live in beatitude. Beatitudes of making the world blessed!

A circulation of shimmers and beatitudes flows in every corner of the earth. A shimmering of light over each inch of the earth. A circularity of blessings, of mutual care, of divine glory. The spark of life in every earthling sparks glory when they act out of care for another, allowing for connection with the Spirit of life, its blessing. Small gestures everywhere: a flow of shimmering divine happenings. Our religious task is to discern the metaphysics of all these shimmering glories, the pantheologies of divine movements that occur at each symbiotic encounter. Vinciane Despret describes the wondrous flow of beatitudes, of these shimmerings:

> Due to the intrinsic interdependence of all existence, the narratives of each living being intertwine, intersect, and write upon each other. Bacteria write their projects on the bodies of their hosts, the birds, on the fruit seeds they carry to enable new encounters, the male bees carry the narratives of the flowers where they collect pollen, and the flowers themselves carry, in the form of incorporated narratives (scents, colors, and shapes), the bees' projects. They all tell stories, in the past, present, and future, to each other and about each other. Therefore, each narrative constitutes a proposition, a bet on the future, a lure for existence, perhaps for metamorphoses. This is also the case with the narrative of the lichen, which carries the narrative of the algae's project, and the algae, carrying the narrative of the lichen, will interpret this narrative, which may modify it, forcing it to invent other stories.[69]

To live in a world filled with these wonders is to live in beatitude, fully blessed, fully happy! Shimmering! To be religious is to be able to see the brilliance of life pulsing in every step. Like grace abounding in every gesture that makes something happy, blessed. We have to keep asking: What world is this in which a singing bird is a divine event? What shimmering glory is that? What world is this where a seed becomes a tree that gives us fruit to eat and live? How can we count such blessings? What world is this when the water of a river flows in me, another body of water? What radiance is this? We must ask these questions amid so much destruction, disintegration, violence and death.

Outside of modernity, where reason is used to explain everything, the singing of a bird, the flourishing of a seed, and the flowing of the water exist in the realm of wonder, of the shimmering divine, the presence of the blessed/Spirit. Yes, we receive these gifts from the spirit/Spirit/s of the land; we share them with each other, with our fellow earthlings; we return it to the spirit/Spirit/s in a reciprocal economy of beatitudes. Our eco-nomos, the law of the eco/oikos, the earth, is not one that tells us to hoard, a mentality built upon scarcity, but is instead one that directs us to share the bountiful blessings, beatitudes, and shimmerings from the earth. It is this economy of beatitudes/shimmerings that keeps the earth alive. These beatitudes/shimmerings go by different names, including within religious traditions.

CHAPTER EIGHT

The Religiosities That Surround Us

Religious people must learn how to engage with animal religions. As Jane Goodall says,

> Often I am asked if the chimpanzees show any signs of religious behavior. I think perhaps their "elemental" displays are precursors of religious ritual. [She then describes study of waterfalls, water watching, and rain dance behaviors she has witnessed.] . . . Is it not possible that these performances are stimulated by feelings akin to wonder and awe?[70]

James B. Harrod asserts that "The patterning of chimpanzee ritual behaviors evidences all the components of a prototypical trans-species definition of religion. These findings support hypotheses that propose religious behaviors for other species, including hominins prior to Homo sapiens sapiens."[71] Chimpanzees create rituals and adapt those rituals' performances, contexts, and meanings. Animals reorient spaces; they pause, they wonder, they do, and repeat events. Despret says that

> All these characteristics—rain dance, enchantment or defiance in the face of the elements of nature in revolt, or in the face of its beauty, behaviors of respect in the face of death, ritualized behavior, etc.—seem to suggest, according to Harrod, that chimpanzees "recognize when they are dealing with an unusual event, one that demands unusual responses"; in short, that they have a religion. However, Harrod clarifies, without theology . . . Would a religion without beings, a religion so depopulated, a religion "addressed to no one"—in some way, an inverted pantheism—still be a religion?[72]

Harrod doesn't try to offer a human sense of religion; as he says, "a trans-species definition of religion does not require such human religious behavior as animism or worship of god(s) to consider the religious dimensions of chimpanzee cognition, affect, and behavior."[73] And Despret also fabulates religious behaviors in Australian wombats: "they realized that there would be 'something else' in this world, 'something else' towards which their creative impulse should be directed."[74] She notes that wombats' feces are cube-shaped—and that with it, they build walls and homes for themselves, shelters that also offer refuge to other animals during forest fires. The animals' very excreta serve a number of purposes: aesthetic, architectural, existential—even, perhaps, theological. Despret says that

> Each wall would then constitute a link in a network whose extent we can only imagine. Or multiple links, each fecal cube itself capable of counting: a theological compound made of seeds, mushrooms, roots, herbs, and bark—the most earthly and immanent transubstantiation that theology could ever have invented. The networks of the wombats' countless galleries would be matched, on the surface, by an equally dense, equally immanent network of organic powers linked to the cosmos. These beings of the depths, these beings of the burrows, would have invented, through their walls, so many ways of connecting the Earth and the cosmos. The walls would then constitute polyphonic narratives, material, chemical, and formal poems, addressed to multiple beings, past and present, perhaps even to beings of the future: they would form a fecal cosmopolitics.[75]

I am not trying to prove that animals have religions, but instead to ask why not? Influenced by Despret, and by the practices of these ritual gestures, I want to ask why some categories or concepts are considered exclusively human. Why not believe that animals are able to do things we don't understand or can't imagine? To believe in this way is to change how we perceive our own thinking and practices. Despret's work both helps us understand how anthropomorphism has guided most animal research, damaging our relationship with the animals we study; and pushes us to move beyond our own anthropocentric ways of thinking about and relating to animals.[76]

Our embassies intended to build relationships with animals must include an interreligious branch, to alert and open us to their unique religious ways, all while being cautious about the possibility of imposing upon them anthropomorphic and anthropocentric reductions. We will have to bring human and animal cosmologies into conversation, allowing the wombats and all other animals, as Despret says, "their own narratives."[77] In the process, we will also be able to see the beatitudes as *religious* presences among us all. Forms of living that lighten and guide our forms of living in, relating to, and orienting ourselves to the many worlds around us.

Beatitudes, then, are circulations of religious behaviors found throughout nature, a state of the body and the mind in relation, the self-realization of being-with, earthlings living and breathing very differently, but together. Beatitudes bless our lives together, bringing new potential, happiness, and thus fullness, infusing our enhanced meetings and connections with respect, power, and protection, contributing to the flow of all of life's encounters.

Blessed are those who are curious about the many forms of life in the places they live.
Blessed be those who pay attention to their surroundings.
Blessed are those who learn about the lives of other beings around them; by learning they start to love them.
Blessed are those who protect refuges for other beings.
Blessed be those who notice all their neighbors, human, and more-than-human.
Blessed be those who stop for an encounter and become responsible to it.
Blessed be those who listen to the birds and attend to the fullness of their lives.
Blessed are those who open their own homes as refuges for all who flee from fire.
Blessed be those who pause to smell a flower.
Blessed be those who know the difference between pests and wild animals, and those who know how weeds serve the soil.
Blessed be those who pollinate the fields so that others may eat.
Blessed be those who stop "development" anywhere.
Blessed be those who cry along with a polluted river.
Blessed be those who have no fear of opossums.
Blessed be those who see every earthling as fundamental to our mutual existence.
Blessed be those who plant flowers and call them by their names.
Blessed be those who fight to stop "growth" intended for the exclusive benefit of humans.
Blessed be those who protect the forests.
Blessed be those who stop to move roadkill.
Blessed be those who can relate to spiders.
Blessed be those who know the desires of the earth.
Blessed be those who live with the seasons and by what their bioregion provides.
Blessed be those who learn to know and love another species.
Blessed be those who fight for every species that is seen as nameless, valueless, meaningless, that is oppressed in and by any type of society.
Blessed be those who include other species in their own thinking, feeling, and living.
Blessed be those who pulse with the glorious animacy and shimmering of life.

Blessed be those who can hear our ancestors speaking to us, and their call to responsibility toward future generations.
Blessed be those who have shed the assumption that the earth is a mechanical object, who now live in the shimmering joy of the unpredictably moving and transforming lives in each of our bioregions.
Blessed be those who feel with all their senses the yes of all living beings, writing poetry, bestowing creations upon the world, so that other beings respond with their own yes to the continuation of life.
Blessed be those who have turned their no into yes so that life may flourish, even those life-forms they do not know or cannot imagine.
Blessed be those who come to know the difference between insects that present real dangers to them and those that will cause them no harm.
Blessed be those who avoid devouring animals, but instead set aside for them refuges and spaces to make their homes.
Blessed be those who reject the need to control, to gain, to win, to have more, and instead find abundance in basic fulfillment of their needs so that other beings, animals, insects, plants, waters, and biomes can also live fully.
Blessed be those who are completely transformed by an encounter with another species.
Blessed be those who listen to the cries of the oppressed and the cries of the earth.
Blessed be those who have learned to lose or to tame their fears of rats, flying foxes, opossums, bats, spiders, and other animals and insects, and have learned that these fellow creatures are not bent on killing them.
Blessed be those who can see the shimmering of life in every corner of the earth, especially in places where we have lost something of great value.
Blessed be those who cry for the children who will never see a rhinoceros or fireflies or any other animal at risk of disappearing from this earth.
Blessed be those able to sense the brilliance of life-forms they don't understand.
Blessed be those who continue to fight for this earth, even when there is little to no reason to believe what they do matters.
. . . To be continued by every reader within their own bioregion.

These beatitudes paint a vision of transformed living—but how do we get there? How do we move from aspiration to action, from blessing to becoming? The answer lies in ritual practice, in the daily gestures that reshape our attention and, through attention, our lives. This is why the three gestures of rising, bowing, and prostrating are not mere symbolic acts but powerful tools of transformation.

CHAPTER NINE

Why a Ritual?

Later in the book, we will go more deeply into the importance of ritual. But for now, it is important to say that rituals can heighten the sense of a moment, our perception of ourselves, and our surroundings. Perhaps the hope of rituals is evident in the desire of Brazilian poet Manoel Bandeira: "May the importance of a thing be measured by the enchantment of what this thing produces in us."[78] More than their functionality, the *attention* rituals awaken within us can lead to all manner of wonder. Our body can experience a heightened sense of the life present in our environment, be it through an object; a movement; or a presence in, under, and/or around us. The ritual proposed in this book is nothing more than an alternative form of attention.

Rituals can make us pay attention and attention can also entail caring. Through rituals, we attend to something, then we admire it, then we care about it—and if we care, we want to know more. That is the path to loving a tree, a bird, a river, a person, or anybody. Once I began paying attention to a opossum, I began to admire how she lived, the way she carried her babies. Before then, her face scared me; now that face is a part of me, a part that I have to care for. And if I am to care for her, I need to know what she eats, what she needs to survive, and how I can provide for and protect her.

I'm telling you about the opossum because now, if I come across dead animals by the side of the road, I often give them a funeral. I once found a dead opossum in the middle of the road, half of her babies still attached to her body. Some of those babies had survived; they were motherless children. But I wept for them all, the entire family. I wept so deeply that strangely enough, I felt, and I'm still embarrassed to say it, that that opossum mother was as important as my own mother. Burying that mother opossum I had never known made me feel as if I were rehearsing the burial of my own mother. I offer this story as a reminder of how fundamental mothers of all species are to us, mothering even us humans.

Rituals, however, are always trying to make the spirit/Spirit/s coincide with the real in our lives but it often, if not always, fails. We need to begin to know the stories, the myths of origin, the living of the spirit/Spirit/s in their places in order to learn the stories, the time and place elements that shape a place. In other words, we need to learn how to know the law of the land and the lore of the land in order to be able to formulate their distinctness, and to unfold their manifold forms of being. It is Lévi-Strauss' notion of the discrete,[79] which takes on mythical thought by creating distinctions, classifications, and binary oppositions (raw/cooked, nature/culture, life/death). It makes the world thinkable by establishing discrete categories. On the other side of this movement is the continuous, the ritual, that which tries to maintain continuity among and within that which is discrete, connecting differences, honoring contradictions, confronting the unknown of the stories and the very ways of being of all these elements. In that way, it attempts to hold the sensing of that place-time in continuity, but it also fails to properly unfold the inscrutability of its manifolds, that is, it can never fully connect myth and rite, thought and practice.

Lévi-Strauss's distinction between the discrete and continuous helps us understand why ritual matters for our climate crisis. Myths create discrete categories (raw/cooked, nature/culture, life/death), making the world thinkable by separating and classifying. But rituals work differently: they seek to restore continuity, to reconnect what has been separated. Our three gestures of rising, bowing, and prostrating are precisely this kind of ritual work—attempting to heal the rupture between humans and earth, between us and the more-than-human world, between our daily lives and the ecological crisis we face. However, rituals never fully succeed in bridging myth and practice, the discrete and the continuous. While rituals always fail, it can be generative failure, one that keeps us practicing, keeps us trying to reconnect.

Another very important note on the relation of rituals and forms of attention: it can go really wrong. Rituals can be harmful and entail forms of attention that will be more damaging than constructive. What we pay attention to, if not constantly corrected and re-oriented, can destroy stories, things, other people, beings, and a whole place. The same holds true for caring, which can also be overbearing. Too much or too little caring can be deeply harmful. Rituals must always be cautionary tales as well, demanding learning, relearning, shifting, and changing ourselves constantly.

Rituals are performances and performances change us. Ritual and performance theorist Richard Schechner confirms that "Performance's subject is transformation: the startling ability of human beings to create themselves, to change, to become—for worse or better—what they ordinarily are not."[80] This concept of transformation became real for me when I began to practice the three-part ritual. I happened to be reading a book that snapped me into an awareness of something I had never heard or thought about: why there are no fruit trees on our streets. Fruit trees can provide people, birds, and other animals with food—but they're too messy, and we don't want to attract wild animals. After I finished reading, and encouraged by my growing ritual awareness, I planted two peach trees and an apple tree in my yard. My spiritual practice is indeed transforming me.

The spiritual practice I am proposing here involves rituals meant to break with the forms of perception and sensibility into which we have been educated. Many of us were never taught to pay attention to our bioregion, to consider plants, animals, and rivers as fundamental parts of ourselves. Even most of the rituals found in our religions orient us toward life with only our god and our people. Those rituals pass by or beyond, sometimes even against, the earth. When we gather indoors for worship, the rituals we practice there are done to encourage faithfulness to a tradition that rarely summons us to attention to other lives outside the building.

Rituals orient our affections; they tell us who and with whom to be; they tell us whom and what to avoid. What this ritual intends to do, then, is to reorient our whole selves (mind, body, emotions) toward our surroundings, the place in which our bodies are present, coming together to shape that space with other beings. This spiritual practice wants to reorient our senses so that we pay attention to the trees, the birds, the flowers, the plants, the wind, and the animals around us. The wish is that our ears hear what we have been deaf to: the sounds of the birds, the whispering of the leaves, the flow of the waters. It is meant to shift our sensitivity as we learn to smell the different aromas within our environment. It wants to do away with our inability to perceive other beings, and teach us to see how we are treating them. A new spiritual life, guided by an entirely new spirit, must include new forms of perception and relation, of and with people and other beings.

In this way, the spiritual practice discussed here aims to open up possibilities of encounter. In *Meeting Mystery*, liturgical theologian Nathan D. Mitchell says that the role of ritual is not to "produce meanings" but "meetings."[81] In these meetings, we realize we are never an I but always a we—an I only if in relation to and enmeshed with thousands of other I's in a very diverse bioregion. If we are to *meet* other beings we will have to abide by rules of diplomacy in order to make contact, to learn about them and become responsible for them.

But our present is filled with such absurdity and sadness that we can easily become paralyzed, unable to see how any of these meetings could matter. This book and the spiritual practice it describes offer one way to respond to that feeling, so that we can find a way to live fully. Remember that ritual gestures entail movement both inward and outward.

Inward because there is work we must do on ourselves. I believe we are all possessed by the demon that goes by the name capitalism. All of us, institutions and individuals, need to cast out this demon, this pervasive force that drives our obsession with money, that causes us to objectify the earth, that alienates us from a fundamental connection to the land. We need a different spirit, and these ritual gestures are meant to cast out the demon of capitalism and to allow us to receive instead the spirit or spirits of the land.

These gestures also work outward, hoping to create connections with people and the earth, to guide us in organizing groups and forming intentional communities that will create new communal gardens, work to protect rivers, demand that polluting industries be shut down, and fight to end our culture of incarceration. Something like Greenpeace joining up with the American Civil Liberties Union (ACLU) to defend both our social and natural worlds.

Very briefly and generally, ritual as I use it here is understood in the following ways:

1 **Ritual as** medicine, mutual sustenance, facilitator of deep connection between the land and each other. In this book, rituals aim in particular to generate deeper correspondence and collaboration with the land, especially with the local terrains in which we live. It hopes to create awareness of all other beings around us, not only of humans but also all other species: trees, plants, rivers, birds, all other animals. In my own professional context, it is as if Union Theological Seminary were to consider its fundamental mission being in relationship with and caring for the Hudson River and the birds, plants, and trees on our campus, all collaborating as essential citizens.

2 **Ritual as** inventor of lifeways and means of survival in this trying time. Rituals may help us foster forms of living, defending, moving, acting, and sparking transformation that finds new ways of caring for the most disadvantaged, our animals, our birds, our local farmers, our rivers, our homeless populations, our bioregion. And as we carry out these smaller-scale actions, we may just set in motion larger processes that bring down vile regimes.

3 **Ritual as** molecular revolution, inventor of forms of resistance and transformation. A term coined by French philosopher Félix Guattari, molecular revolution is a double movement that fractures capitalism in general and our individual and collective lifestyles. By calling attention to the correlation between social and subjective transformation, Guattari says that micropolitics and molecular revolutions are powerful means of enacting the changes we need. He says:

> Yes, I believe that there is a multiple people, a people of mutants, a people of potentialities that appears and disappears, that is embodied in social events, literary events, and musical events. I'm often accused of being exaggeratedly, stupidly, stubbornly optimistic, and of not seeing people's wretchedness. I can see it, but . . . I don't know, perhaps I'm raving,

but I think that we're in a period of productivity, proliferation, creation, utterly fabulous revolutions from the viewpoint of this emergence of a people. That's molecular revolution: it isn't a slogan or a program, it's something that I feel, that I live, in meetings, in institutions, in affects, and also through some reflections.[82]

Ritual as molecular revolution is this plethora of movements not only within literature but everywhere people relate to the earth in transformative ways. It is this feeling/doing/living/reflecting/affecting together to transform ourselves and the planet—combined efforts about which we will learn more later in the book.

FIGURE 3 *Rooted life.*

CHAPTER TEN

An Aesthetic Movement

The idea is simple: if I can relate to the birds, the trees, and the rivers around me in a daily ritual focused on correlating different subjectivities, I may become more aware of the world and its needs, and thus more inclined to join with others in protecting and caring for those nearby birds, trees, and rivers. In that work of informed caring, we come to see that capitalism is killing those trees, birds, and rivers—and is destroying in the process the very ways I and we all move about in the world. Rituals, then, help us tie together seemingly distant fields—whether those fields are literal or disciplinary—and possible actions that had previously been unable to cooperate. In the words of ritual theorist Tom Driver, the power and purpose of ritual "is to assist the dynamic of social change through ritual processes of transformation."[83]

A necessary caution comes from my Buddhist friends Xian'an and Xian'ai: while rituals are skillful means and can help us create, imagine, and do so many things, they are not ends in themselves. As isolated, self-contained practices, whether we're speaking about rituals in general or the particular one I describe here, rituals are of little use. In other words, we should not cling to any form of ritual; doing so means destroying both the ritual itself and the potential it contains. The structure of ritual includes a fundamental element of flexibility that allows each particular ritual to be done in whatever fashion the person carrying it out might choose. Additionally, that ritual can act as a springboard, introducing whatever other ritual that is needed in a certain place. Anyone can engage in the ritual as originally offered, change it, expand it, and/or leave it behind. The essential thing to remember is that we must not cling to it as an immovable whole, or fetishize any of its aspects; otherwise, it will lose its power.

It should be no surprise, then, that every religious tradition can work with the gestures I describe in this book in the way they feel is appropriate. In some ways, the ritual can be practiced as is within set systems of beliefs, or its contents/form adapted to needed structures. But it might also be used as a way of expanding, transforming, and even changing one's existing belief system. What is at stake in all of these situations, though, is the need to listen and to connect with the Earth; it is the Spirit of the Earth to whom we must carefully attend. I am guided by the thought of Amazonian Yanomami Xaman Davi Kopenawa, who said soon after the height of the Covid pandemic:

> I am a shaman and I am not alone. Only shamans know the vision of the future of Brazil and the world. T+t+ri [Forest Spirit] communicates with shamans. We are connected to the land and the forest. All of us, the people of the planet, will suffer, as we are already suffering. Our world, planet Earth, is under complete threat . . . The world is full of problems. The city people think the planet is fine, but deep down, we who talk to T+t+ri know that it is not. Planet Earth is crying out, asking for help so that the forest can be protected. The city people cannot hear Mother Earth's cry for help.[84]

This ritual is intended to help all of us hear "Mother earth's cry for help." If we listen, we will hear the demand to change everything within ourselves and around us: our personal beliefs, perceptions, and modes of living. In other words, our way of organizing our society in general: our educational systems, our economies, our religions, and so on.

This book is also a work of aesthetics; that is, it points to the ways we discern and depict the world using the particular forms and structures constitutive of our senses. Here, "aesthetic" does not rely only on the sense of what is beautiful or just; instead, it is a fundamental way of reorienting the sensible order of our collective lives, whether natural, economic, social, or political. The beautiful and the just are there, then—but so too are the ugly and the unjust. In other words, the idea is to expand the ways we understand our lives, to call our attention to the interrelationality in which we are embedded and according to which we live every day. Paul B. Preciado defines aesthetics as it relates to *petrosexoracial aesthetics*: "By aesthetics, I mean the articulation between the social organization of life, the structure of perception and the configuration of a shared sensory experience. The aesthetic always depends on a political regulation of the sensory apparatus of the living body in a society."[85]

Our senses are at the heart of the aesthetic, and this book wants to expand our awareness of the interrelation between our bodies and our political, social, racial, sexual, religious, and ecological orientations. This awareness can help us foster a much larger sense of agency, belonging, political possibility, and mode of living, along with a rediscovery of many wonders ultimately able to change all of our lives.

This is a very simple book. Its only hope is to ignite something that will help us live more fully, more joyfully, and perhaps face up to the challenges of our times. Religion is not providing us the tools we now need, and we are all perishing. We must create new rituals for unprecedented times; our beliefs, practices, and manners of thinking and feeling must change.

Gil Anidjar once wrote a message for me in one of his books: "Remembering, Remembering, and Remembering. There is mothering in that." Perhaps the gestures I describe are all about remembering. Remembering the skies, remembering every species and spirit around us, and remembering the land. For if we do that, we will *re-member* that the earth has been mothering creation long before we even got here and will continue to mother it long after we are gone. My hope is that this ritual will help us see and feel that we are mothered by the earth, right here and now. But now let us spend some time with some definitions.

CHAPTER ELEVEN

Bioregion and Other Terms

Before we continue, let me clarify the words I use here in relation to the concept of a bioregion. For me, terms such as nature, habitat, environment, biome, landscape, neighborhood, patch of land, territory, and bioregion are interchangeable throughout the book. Each of these words, though, has its own specificity, conceptual use, history, and forms of relating to other concepts. When I use these words interchangeably, I do not want to conflate them, or convey a sense that they are synonyms. Instead, I bring them into the conversation as a very loose way of using different terms to help us understand and relate to the unique places in which we live, small territories and not the earth as a whole.

I also use the word "nature" in two ways: first, in the very broad, more common sense that many people have: "uninhabited" landscapes that include countryside, forests, wilderness, biomes, parks, and so on. City dwellers often say they need to go out into nature to breathe different air. Thus, nature here seems to be the contrary, or the opposite, of culture, of cities, of highly populated areas in which it is hard to see "nature." However, we must insist that nature is everywhere we are, whether in Times Square or in any downtown area's traffic-filled streets. Because we *are* nature, we could say that *everything* is nature: people, other species, buildings, asphalt, houses, and so on.

But this notion of nature is also problematic. Here, the concern in particular is with modernity's understanding of nature,[86] in which God is replaced by nature, and nature is something we fear or of which we are in awe. It is a place of either ugliness, populated by beasts and general unruliness, or of tidy beauty, a place filled with either pure abstraction or pure materiality. These understandings of nature are too generalized, and make it difficult for us to relate to the land. Some people are even opposed to the word nature, viewing it as a problematic concept for environmental philosophy.[87] In this book, though, the idea is to blur all these binaries that fall on one side or the other of the nature/culture divide, to show that each term is part of the other and can't be fully separated; each belongs to and with each other. For example, every cultural decision has to do with nature, and nature defines our cultural habits. In the same vein, we could say that every political decision is an ecological decision, and every ecological decision is also fully political.

Anna Lowenhapt Tsing understands nature in three ways:

> Imagine "first nature" to mean ecological relations (including humans) and "second nature" to refer to capitalist transformations of the environment . . . . My book then offers "third nature," that is, what manages to live despite capitalism. To even notice third nature, we must evade assumptions that the future is that singular direction ahead. Like virtual particles in a quantum field, multiple futures pop in and out of possibility; third nature emerges within such temporal polyphony. Yet progress stories have blinded us. To know the world without them, this book sketches open-ended assemblages of entangled ways of life, as these coalesce in coordination across many kinds of temporal rhythms.[88]

We live within these three natures, and this book tries to raise awareness of all three. But how? First, by bringing us to the realization that we live in first nature—that is, that we do form part of ecological relations. Then, by calling our attention to second nature: the fact that capitalism is transforming and killing us all. Finally, by showing us how to live in third nature, taking us deep within these "open-ended assemblages of entangled ways of life" that emerge and continue to shimmer in many directions, even when the ruins of capitalism, social destruction, and ecological devastation are apparent all around. The three gestures I describe are aimed at bringing us through first and second nature and taking us into full life in third nature. These practices intend to help us learn, in the words of a book Anna Lowenhaupt Tsing coedited, the *Arts of Living on a Damaged Planet*.[89]

That being said, let's focus on the concept of bioregion. The term has its roots in the early 1970s. First used in an academic paper in 1971 by marine biologist E. Jarowski, it was actually coined by Allen Van Newkirk and then popularized by writers like Peter Berg and Raymond Dasmann, who advocated for defining a region by its biogeological boundaries instead of political or social borders. The Planet Drum group of scholars soon emerged, and they defined the term more explicitly:

> A bioregion is a distinct area with coherent and interconnected plant and animal communities, and natural systems, often defined by a watershed. A bioregion is a whole "*life-place*" with unique requirements for human inhabitation so that it will not be disrupted and injured.[90]

Initially understood as defining areas of smaller scale, and only related to the biological composition of a given territory, the concept of a bioregion grew and took on greater nuance. Today, there are more than "25 biotic (biological) approaches to defining bioregions within the context of scientific literature."[91] Over time, the terms bioregion and bioregionalism started to combine the geobiological boundaries of a bioregion with the political and social structures of a local place, aiming at understanding a bioregion as a combined "cultural and natural" structure, considering not only the lives of plants, animals, rivers, geological formations, and so on but also human actions, local culture, and local economies, all of which organize the local environment. In fact, the law and the lore of the land are considered part of a bioregion, encouraging us to consider how all species live together within a certain environment. Today, the concept of bioregion is part of many US university curricula, such as environmental and natural sciences, social sciences, and humanities, and is used in various ways.

It is important to note that the term "bioregion" appears at the same point at which the United States Environmental Protection Agency (EPA) was established. While the EPA uses the term "ecoregion" the concept is now used almost synonymously with bioregion. For example, in the book I do not use the term "biome," which denotes a much larger area (an entire desert, for instance) than a bioregion or ecoregion, which fit within biomes. A term that is closely related to bioregion for me is the concept used by Anna Lowenhaupt Tsing and her colleagues: "patch of land."[92] But there are differences. "Bioregion" tends to convey the sense of a region of any scale that is self-contained. While a patch of land may be considered a delimited territory, it may also be found as a discontinuous "offshoot" in other parts of the world.

For our purposes, I am using the term bioregion more specifically according to the way deep ecology sociologist Bill Devall describes it: "Bio means life and region means the territory or lifeworld of experience. Literally, then, a bioregion is the territory of lived experience, the territory with which a person, or a community of people, identifies as part of their self."[93]

Thus, bioregion designates all of the movements of life and death that happen in a particular location that is marked by geological, biological, and ecological specificities, composed with the sociological, political, racial, economic, class, and gender markers. It should be emphasized that every bioregion includes more than physical features or geographical boundaries: human and nonhuman lifeways; histories of life and death, flourishing and genocide, slavery, displacement, and oppression. Each of us can tap into the many ways our particular bioregion is organized, divided, and understood, seeing then the ways in which everything within a bioregion belongs to it: the law and the lore of the land and the ways the land and that lore extend and enter into relationship with other areas.

Bioregion is then an environment, the patch of land, the grounds within which small and large portions of our braided selves with other beings make the place moving and alive: our memories, our family, our ancestors, our feelings, our experiences, our paradoxes, our doubts, our crises, our aging, our love life, our sorrows, our nourishment—from food to stories, from water to symbols to animals and trees, the entirety of our natural-cultural worlds. All of this is included in my conception of bioregion, which helps us go deep into our respective, present or even future, home grounds.

Within the bioregion, there are neighborhoods where we belong or need to approach more meaningfully. What if we consider every one of our bioregion's species a neighbor? Similar to the way that Saint Francis of Assisi called to brother Sun and Sister Moon, as we walk through our bioregion, we must ask where we can find our neighbors, the birds, the opossums, bees, rivers, mountains, plants, insects, water, air, seeds, soil, fruits, and so on. In doing so, the bioregion becomes a home for us all to share.

CHAPTER TWELVE

Bioregion

Preparation for the Spiritual Practices

No authentic spiritual practice can be carried out without the earth's participation, for we are made of earth. No discrete self untouched by the earth can be found. The practice I describe in this book requires the inward and outward movements I discussed earlier.

As we connect with the land, it will be the land's spirit that will transform our thoughts and feelings, and will cast out the demons of disconnection, of hoarding, of private property. As we connect with the land, our numbness to the theft of the wealthy will dissipate, and we will rise up together to protect the earth and all its beings. As we connect outwardly with the land, we also turn inward. The land reorients our inner life and gives us a sense of who we are: the earth.

These two movements are both the same and different. As we move inwardly, we start to understand that the singing of the birds is not only their singing but ours as well. When we turn to the sea, we turn to the vastness that we ourselves are. When we turn to the rivers, we turn to the water in the wombs of our mothers and the water of which our bodies are made. When we sit in the forest, we turn inside to understand we too are forests. With these realizations, we start to sync our movements with the movements of the earth, coming to see ourselves as part of a larger landscape. When that happens, we realize that there is so much more to existence than work, progress, and personal accomplishment. We become wonder! When we attend to a seed, we learn that it takes a whole year for it to flourish into a blossom before it sends out fruit; that understanding might help us slow down and walk softly on the land. The inward/outward movements into the land/ourselves can help us process our history, our feelings, our emotions, our ways of being.

Some readers, I know, will be concerned about the dangers of anthropomorphism—and they are right to be troubled at the ways humans project our own forms of understanding and feeling onto the natural world. Starting out, though, we must use the language we have and our particular forms of comprehension, running the risk of anthropomorphizing everything. But as we begin to establish relationships with other beings—trees, plants, animals, terrains—we will grow into better ways of interacting and living.[94] As I said before, our connection will instill in us a desire to learn. As we strive to see the fullness of life that is present in each being, we may also make out the presence there of a spirit particular to that being, moving about and claiming a territory. These forms of knowledge are present in the wisdom of Indigenous Peoples in your area.

My story of learning to pay attention reveals a possibility we'll now explore more deeply: this book and the spiritual practice it describes provide a beginner's way of eventually moving into a wiser and much deeper relationship with the land. Even starting out, though, the more we know about our landscape, the life that is present in our bioregion, the more we can learn about ourselves in relation to it. In fact, this exercise is all about listening—not only to the sounds of the human world but also to those made throughout the earth, the noise of all the planet's species. Soundscape ecologist Bernie Krause warns us that at present, "wildlife accounts for only 4 percent of the global biomass, while human beings, livestock, and pets make up the remaining 97 percent. A quarter of all species face extinction, many within decades. The decline is acutely evident through the loss of the natural soundscape."[95] Listening not only to what is present, but also to and for the absences that permeate the world around us, is an exercise that entails focus—and more so, devotion. My intention is that the gestures I describe will aid us in that deep listening, which requires, as Robin Wall Kimmerer specified, intention, and attention.

Anne Bogart, theater director and professor at Columbia University, relating a story that acting teacher Stella Adler shared with her students, helps us think about intention as centered upon trying. "In the *trying*," Bogart interprets Adler saying to her group of would-be, likely frightened, actors, "we attempt a miracle."[96] Our listening, then, is an attempt to make a miracle happen: to fully understand, to give ourselves completely to what we are listening to or for. But listening is also about paying attention—close attention—which means caring deeply. Bogart knows this as well: "The quality and depth of one's attention is ultimately what counts most in every situation. Attention is, after all, one of the few aspects of life that one can control. The only gift we can give to a situation is the force of our attention."[97] Care is the result of both intention and attention.

The ritual I describe in the book is a way of putting into practice the five Rs present in Indigenous Knowledges: respect, relevance, reciprocity, responsibility, and relationships. It helps you *respect* the entire terrain that surrounds you, as well as the beings within it: plants, animals, insects, rivers, trees, birds, soil, flowers, and more. Every being is alive and deserves to be respected and honored. Each being is deeply *relevant* to that environment and needs to be understood in *relation* to everything around it. To learn the relevance of each being is to learn the wisdom that each being carries. That mutual relation calls us to *reciprocate* with each other, knowing that we are all part of a chain of life that depends upon mutual gifts of care and gratitude. The response to this expansive relationship will take the shape of *responsibility*, or as Donna Haraway calls it, "response-ability."[98] Together, the Rs build in us a deep awareness that we are not just building relationships; we essentially *are* relationships. This understanding cannot but help impact our sense of place, our comprehension that a place is unique, and that it requires specific knowledge in order to live within it. This sort of understanding is what we need to engage ourselves in our particular landscapes.

Each of us must go, then, into our own bioregion and understand this place we live, how old it is, and how it has changed over years and even eons, who has lived here and lives here right now, and what forces within it have oriented and continue to orient our common life together. Perhaps there, in our particular bioregion, pausing, listening, watching, and paying attention, we can respond to all its questions. Professor Larry Rasmussen in his book *Earth Honoring Faith* quotes Norman Habel, a scholar of biblical wisdom and the questions he asks: "Have you ever wondered why a frog always jumps like a frog and never runs like an ant? Have you ever been fascinated by the way a baby bird learns to fly as a bird rather than swim like an eel?" Rasmussen explains that "It's the sort of question Wisdom's sages ask: What is the nature of each creature, why is it so, and what might we learn in its presence? Is there some essential and instinctual structure, some internal impulse, that mediates insight for our own ways?"[99]

The structure Rasmussen names is cultural knowledge of a bioregion. Within that knowledge of your bioregion, you are called to learn everything about the place. And living within and in knowledge of the place you inhabit, you are increasingly able to see new forms of relationship, as well as meaning within the universe. When we watch a frog jump, we are not only increasing "scientific" or "objective" knowledge of the bioregion, although that type of knowledge is very important. It is more than that. When we learn how the frog jumps, we also come to understand how the animal lives in that environment: its habits and needs and the roles it plays. We come to understand how we can enter into a relationship with this creature, a relationship in which we humans, as guardians of this bioregion, will be able to assume responsibility for the being in front of us, rather than watching from a distance the phenomenon of a single jumping amphibian. When we stop to wonder "why a frog always jumps like a frog and never runs like an ant," we are trying to understand both why the frog jumps and why the ant walks, so that we can find a way of establishing a necessary relationship between us all—between neighbors. That relational form of mutual belonging and reciprocity is what knowledge of a bioregion is all about: a composition of many knowledges that come along with that locality's many worlds.

The existence of each creature depends upon an entire world; that creature can only survive if it lives in relationship with other creatures within a unique web that defines its native ecology. Thus, building up a robust general knowledge of a bioregion, with all of its animals, insects, fungi, mosses, trees, waters, birds, plants, frogs, ants, humans, and so on, requires understanding a multiplicity of "smaller" knowledge, which are entire worlds, that shape and contribute to that bioregion: every bioregion possesses a law and lore of the land. For Aboriginal Australian author and professor Tyson Yunkaporta, there is no distinction between cultural and natural knowledge of a bioregion. If we are to have that knowledge, he says that we must consider locatedness, relatedness, embodiment, orality, narrative, and image. It is especially important for our purposes to attend to what Yunkaporta says about locatedness:

> In Indigenous culture, no information can exist unless it is located. The knower is always located within a map of knowledge and story that is profoundly place-based and corresponds with real landscapes. The paths and habitual routes throughout the knower's landscape are storied and visualized from a bird's-eye view perspective. Each point of interest on a path of travel represents part of a story and a repository for knowledge. As Aunty Mary says, "I am located, therefore I am."[100]

We see here an intense appeal to go out into your bioregion and learn about it—or in the words of Aunty Mary, to learn who you are. Begin this process by pondering, paying attention to, giving yourself time to learn about, and investigating your landscape, your bioregion. Being able to answer the bioregion quiz included toward the end of this section will help you relate to the book's three gestures and to expand your sense of self.

We can think about a bioregion in a number of ways. Let us check some of these ways.

Bioregion as patch: Anna Lowenhaupt Tsing

We can understand bioregion as a patch of land. Anna Lowenhaupt Tsing defines it this way:

> Patches show us landscape structure, that is, morphological patterns in which humans and nonhumans are arranged. A forest, a city, or

> a plantation: each of these is a landscape structure. We recognize these landscape structures through observations, comparisons, and attunements; landscape structures may be analyzed as part of systems, whether cosmologies, ecological models, or political economies, but they need not be.[101]

However, we have to understand the land, or any patch of land, within the rubric of the *Anthropocene*, a disputed term that characterizes our geological age based on the claim that it is now human activity that is the most dominant influence upon the movement and existence of the earth, including its climate and the entangled existence of all its beings. Anna Lowenhaupt Tsing coins the phrase *patchy Anthropocene*, asserting that "three kinds of systems-thinking come into play for their importance to understanding 'patchy Anthropocene': ecological models, nonsecular cosmologies, and political economies."[102] In discussing the confluence of these forms of systems-thinking, she mentions the place of Spirits within the patchy Anthropocene. Here, they are the fundamental presences that both orient and disorient the order and flux of each place—and we all—teachers, practitioners, thinkers, writers, and everyone else—should pay attention to the Spirits present within each patch of land:

> Spirits might be models that have a habit of escaping the systems out of which they emerge. They invite us to unpredict these systems in surprising ways. Spirits may close high-tech airports, affect democratic elections, or aid scientific discovery . . . . At the very historical juncture where modern reason declared spirits and monsters to be dead, the graphs of the Great Acceleration (Steffen et al. 2015) have helped draw the contours of the uncanny valleys of the Anthropocene in which the spirits and monster dwell . . . . . In this sense, anthropologists need to take natural science models as seriously as spirits. Doing so means neither taking them naively for granted nor dismissing them out of hand as cultural construction.[103]

Anna Lowenhaupt Tsing's patchy Anthropocene helps us think about the concept of bioregion. But we can also look at the idea of working in line with Christian liberation theologies, whose demand that we ask *where we are* differentiates them from other types of theological investigation. Here, the recognition is explicit that theology arises out of the places we live, the people we live with, the connections between us, the allegiances we have established, and the sides we take. In other words, theology has to do with Jesus's assertion that "where your treasure is, there will your heart be also."[104] "There" is the "where" under consideration in the bioregion, in the cosmology of *territorial* liberation theologies.

Territory and interdependence: Bruno Latour

In the same way, Bruno Latour wrestles in *After Lockdown* with the question, "Where am I?"[105] To understand where I am, I need to understand my territory, which would be another way of understanding a bioregion. But understanding a territory is not easy. As Latour says, "Territory is not what you occupy. It's what defines you."[106] The definition is deceptively simple; Latour provides further detail about what is actually a very complex way of understanding the notion of territory:

> "Let's try and situate ourselves in a spot we'll need to try and describe in tandem with others." Surprising association of verbs: to subsist, to make a group, to be on a particular patch of soil, to describe oneself . . . Describing a territory the wrong way round and from above, as we know, means consulting a map, locating a point at the intersection of abscissae and ordinates . . . (or follow) a grid of coordinates, but by answers to questions about interdependence. What do I depend on to subsist; what are the threats that weigh on that which provides for me; what confidence can I have in those who tell me about those threats; what do I do to protect myself against them; what are the aids I might find to help me extricate myself; who are the opponents I have to try to contain? These questions, too, draw up a territory, but the drawing produced doesn't tally with the previous manner of getting our bearings. Being tracked is not the same thing as situating oneself; in both cases, what is measured is indeed what counts, but it doesn't count in the same way.[107]

A territory can also be explained by the notion of the *local* we have been talking about in this book. A territory or locality is defined by a notion of interdependency. Territory is not only defined or circumscribed by a map, an arbitrary drawing in an urban setting, or marked off by fences, but rather, a territory, or the local, is whatever is connected through relations of *interdependence* between earthlings, established by relations of mutual need, belonging, and dependence. For example, I am dependent on the water I drink, which sends me out in search of where the water comes from, in which lake or river it originates. At the same time, I have to know the places this river is located, a knowledge that includes those places' histories. Along the way, I have to understand who depends upon this water: fish, people, birds, vegetation, and others. In this way, my territory or my locality is established not by an arbitrarily defined bioregion; instead, the bioregion is defined by the patterns, traces, and fluctuations of the river that pours into my glass from my tap.

I must confess that Latour's question—"Where am I?"— gets me to a point where I cannot fully answer it. I realize that I didn't know the name of the river my drinking water came from. I didn't know which birds were native to my neighborhood or which trees had been here before colonial settlement. This ignorance wasn't innocent; it was the product of an education that taught me everything except how to know my own place. Learning my bioregion has meant unlearning this disconnection, one river, one tree, one bird at a time. I have yet so many ways to go.

Obligations of place: Isabelle Stengers

A local place or a territory is also inherently marked by *obligations* and demands. Bruno Latour cites Isabelle Stengers's notion of obligations: "the more precise your description becomes, the more it obligates you. Coming down to earth doesn't mean going local—in the sense of the usual metrics. It means being able to encounter the beings we depend on, however far away they may be in kilometers."[108] That means that I am obligated to make sure the river my water comes from is well treated, preserved, cared for, and kept alive. In other words, the local is essentially what is common to me and to others, including the river. This notion of a territory or a bioregion, then, explodes the binaries of near and far, local and universal. Bruno Latour says:

> But once it's put back the right way round, we call "local" what is discussed and argued in common. "Near" doesn't mean "a few kilometres away," but "what attacks me or provides for me in a direct way"; it's a measure of commitment and intensity. "Distant" doesn't mean "far away in kilometres," but whatever you don't have to worry about straightaway because it has no involvement in the things you depend on. Consequently, what you bring together in your description is neither local nor global, but put together according to a different relationship of concatenation with entities you're going to have to confront one by one, maybe at the cost of countless polemics.[109]

Planetary and territorial: Dipesh Chakrabarty

Thus, to discover, or "re-enter" our territory, is to critically consider who we are in relation to whom we live with, belong to, and need to survive. This consideration is nothing less than a huge process of transformation, of metamorphosis, where we reevaluate what we think, understand, feel, and imagine about where *we live* and how we are situated on our planet. It is both a process of exhaling and inhaling both the planet and the territory we live in and belong to. On the one hand, we consider the planet. As Dipesh Chakrabarty says, we live on a planet, one that has various histories: the history of the planet itself, the history of the life of the planet, and the history of the globe: that is, the story of capital, of empires, and technology.[110]

This is how we must approach a larger understanding of our life on this planet, as a collection of beings living together, changing and transforming one another.

This kind of territorial knowledge can feel overwhelming. How can I possibly learn the planetary history, the life history, and the colonial history of my place? But we can start small: with one question, one walk, one conversation at a time with someone who knows this land better than I do. Each small place of the bioregion has somebody who is an expert on that patch of land. The point is not necessarily to become an expert ourselves but to learn with those local people who are experts and learn, change ourselves, become attentive, engaged.

These voices—Anna Lowenhaupt Tsing, Bruno Latour, Isabelle Stengers, and Dipesh Chakrabarty—converge on a crucial insight: understanding where we are is not a matter of coordinates on a map but of tracing webs of interdependence and obligation. A bioregion or territory is defined not by boundaries but by relationships: what we depend on, what depends on us, and what we're obligated to protect. For our purposes, this means that our three ritual gestures cannot be done abstractly or generically. Rising, bowing, and prostrating only become meaningful when they're practiced in response to *this particular* river, *these specific* trees, *our actual* neighbors—human and more-than-human. The ritual works precisely because it forces us to ask, again and again: Where am I? Who shares this place with me? What do I depend on to survive?

On the other hand, we must understand that within this grand planetary conception, we live in a territory, a bioregion, a local place. The confluence of the planetary and the territorial orients the very question: *Where am I?* This question is at the heart of our spiritual search, since it demands we be fully reinstated in the place, according to particular ways of living. The spiritual quest of determining *where we are,* since the I is always a certain we, has to do with each of our existential, cosmological, cultural/natural concerns and spiritual relations, interconnections, and obligations with the many beings around us. Thus, the spiritual gestures offered in this book hope to help us delve deeply into that constant question of *where we are,* holding fast to a vision of the necessary, unavoidable metamorphosis and movement we require: namely, plunging into our territories and changing our assumptions about *living on* a place into an understanding of *living off* of a place where so many beings live and are dependent upon each other.[111]

This process will eventually bring us to the realization that our earth is finite and that we cannot survive by pursuing exponential growth year after year. How can governments establish the goal of annual economic growth of 3, 4, or 5 percent when the earth itself does not grow according to such a scale? The politics of care and interdependence that Latour talks about have to do with the establishment of limits, reorientation of our living, awareness of forms of connection, engendering modes of care for every thread of life that we depend on, and deep responsibility for all beings and entire territories.

But for us to do that, we also must understand the need to restore a form of relationship with the animal and plant worlds that we have long shunned. The forms of spiritual life established by various religions shut down the voices of nonhuman beings in order to listen only to the human voice as God's privileged channel. Emanuele Coccia, discussing the work of Bruce Albert and Davi Kopenawa, clarifies this separation: "If the religions adopted by the West preferred to focus on the history of a clear and absolute division with the animal world, if they made the human a superior species superior to all others, it was to attenuate the tragedy of the incommunicability between them."[112]

This means that we need to reinstitute a means of communicating between ourselves and the worlds of flora and fauna. Of the many ways Indigenous Amazonians continue to maintain a very strong relationship with these worlds, one is listening. That listening has resulted in the establishment and preservation of a deep connection to plants and animals, a connection that allows them to understand other beings' movements and habits. In turn, this understanding means the region's Indigenous communities are simultaneously able to hunt for food and safeguard a thriving shared life with all inhabitants of the rainforest.

We, though, have lost this ability to hear, an ability our journey into ritual gestures is meant to recover. Along the way, we will surely romanticize this and other abilities and customs, and will make many mistakes. But perhaps the more we learn about our connections to a territory, the more our obligations to our fellow creatures within the territory will be revealed. With time, we may learn their languages, understand their habits, and realize how our lifestyles have interfered with, challenged, and changed their behaviors. Our growing knowledge may then allow us to provide them with greater care, better and more intentional protection, and as-yet unimagined ways of supporting these species' flourishing. In the process, we can flourish as well. Coccia offers some thoughts on moving forward with our efforts:

> First of all, animals have no moral superiority over us: life in all its forms is ambiguous and will continue to be so. That is why it is necessary to know the world, to question other species, and to seek the best alliance with them. On the other hand, referring to animals and plants never means referring to an absence of history, to a world without culture or technology. It is about entering into a relationship with an infinity of mediations, as is the case every time we enter into a relationship with another human being. Contrary to what we have believed, the problem is not the lack of consciousness or speech of other species, but our inability to perceive them. All animals and all living beings speak, but we have not yet found the Rosetta Stone that translates their language into ours.

> That is why, to the thesis of incommunicability between humans and non-humans, this book opposes that of a "humanimal polyglotism."[113]

We must become proficient—maybe even fluent—in this *humanimal polyglotism* as we plunge into our territories, bioregions, and neighborhoods. The gestures I have been describing will help us approach other species, hopefully sparking within us the desire to learn more about them. The more we know, the closer to these others we will feel; the less fear we will have of them, the greater our admiration for them will be, the better our care, and the more devoted our love. That is the ritual's intended itinerary. The hope is that this ritual will allow us to begin this process, helping us to see what a great distance we have kept between ourselves and other species, how inextricably our lives actually are with theirs—and then begin to undo this self-created division. The initial small steps of rising, bowing, and touching the ground can lead to gradual daily change, ultimately helping us live fully both on and off of our territories through complex forms of care, interaction, and mutual flourishing.

CHAPTER THIRTEEN

One More Round

Yunkaporta provides some suggestions for how to attain greater cultural knowledge of a bioregion:

1. The knower creates symbolic maps of the routes they travel regularly in the places they live.
2. The knower translates the information they wish to remember into stories and encodes these stories onto their maps.
3. The knower creates phrases utilizing rhyme, repetition, alliteration, and taboo language and content to enhance memory at different stages of the story map.
4. The knower creates objects and images (or both, inscribing images on the objects) that reference maps or parts of maps as memory aids.
5. The knower creates these things in collaboration with others who are learning the same information, forming deep relationships that keep the memories together.[114]

It may be helpful to follow these steps in investigating your own environment, which will in turn help you answer the short bioregion quiz below. Responding to that quiz will help you begin to pay attention to your surroundings: to relate to, know, admire, care for, change, belong to, and become responsible for them. To love the world around you. The quiz is very short compared to many of the extensive bioregion quizzes available online (a few of which I've included in the notes, and I encourage you to further test your understanding of your area using them)—but in answering the questions it asks, you will begin to get an idea of what is involved in really knowing your surroundings.[115] Following the quiz, I offer some thoughts about how to relate those questions and others I have added to the spiritual practice described in the book.

Once you have learned something about your bioregion, find the Indigenous communities that have lived there for ages. Learn their histories and stories; ask if you would be welcome at their events and festivities. Learn their names for the beings around you; discover what they understand by the concept spirit; take note of how they orient their lives according to the needs and patterns of the land.

All of this theory matters because it reframes a simple question: Where am I? But theory begets practice—only intimate knowledge of your particular place can do that. The following quiz will help you begin discovering what you know and don't know about your bioregion, revealing where you need to deepen your attention and relationship.

FIGURE 4 *Habitat.*

CHAPTER FOURTEEN

Understanding Your Bioregion

A Brief Quiz

1 Take a walk. In the fields around you, in the local parks or on neighbors' and businesses' lawns, which native species are growing? Which are nonnative to the area—and which are invasive?

2 How many trees can you name in your neighborhood? Do you know which ones are native to your region?

3 Where does the water you use come from? Water connects you to a network of life—human and more-than-human—that depends on the same rivers and aquifers. Where does it end up when it goes down the drain or flows off the lawn?

4 What is the average amount of precipitation you get in your region each year? Each month? At present, where do you stand in comparison to this average? Has that average changed over the last five years? The last ten?

5 How good are the air and water quality in your neighborhood? What are the main sources of air and water pollution there, and who is responsible for monitoring and regulating sources of pollution?

6 Who picks up your garbage? Where does it go from there? How is it sorted? Where does it end up?

7 What types of birds live in your area? How long do they remain in your neighborhood during the year? What are their migration patterns? Which bird is the first to arrive in spring?

8 How dark is your neighborhood at night? Can you see the stars? Is there any awareness of or effort to cut down on light pollution?

Do you know how light pollution affects birds' migration patterns?

9 How do you heat and cool your home? Does the energy that powers your home come from gas, oil, electric, or solar? Who determines what options you have in powering your home?

10 Where does your food come from? Where is it grown or raised? Who cultivates, harvests, slaughters, transports, pays for, and is paid—and how?—for your food?

11 Do you know which hardiness zone you live in? What is the growing season in your area? How is that different from other areas? Do you eat food grown within your region?

12 Do you know what types of soil are in your neighborhood? Which types of flowers and other plants flourish in your region?

13 Which wild animals are common in your area? Is their habitat being threatened, and if so, by what types of human activity? How many animals are killed every year by cars?

14 Without relying on signs, roads, or anything constructed by people, provide directions to your home.

15 Who are the animals and plants that have learned to survive urban environments? Pigeons, stray cats and dogs, ants, squirrels, trees, grass, plants, "weeds," and more. Where do they live? What do they eat, and what do they drink? What if you were to start imagining the urban world from the perspective of these animals and plants? What is it like to live there and what does it take to survive on their own in a world of humans?

16 How has the appearance and use of the land where you live changed over the last hundred years?

17 What is the current phase of the moon? How does the moon affect Earth and the beings who live in and on it?

After you have gone through this list, give yourself time to learn about, conduct research on, and engage yourself in your region. Now, as you stand outside your home, answer the following questions and take the following actions.

Question

What kinds of trees live in your neighborhood? Are they native? If not, where did they come from? Are all these trees good for the environment? Why are they there: for decoration? For the life of the community? Why don't we create a mini-community of beings centered around fruit trees? Is there any spirit you can relate to that you have felt on your own or that you know of thanks to the region's Indigenous People?

Connect

Offer a glass of water and words of gratitude to a nearby tree. Start a conversation with the tree. Is it a he, a she, a they? If you don't want to assume its gender, try to treat the tree as a subject, as a full living being, as a somebody. It's not what you hear that's important, but what you say. Spend some time with the tree, and as you leave, honor it. You can both rise and bow to this tree.

Question

What type of vegetation lives in your area? Which plants live in your region; what types of flowers are nearby? Which crops are seasonal, and who are the area's local farmers you can support? Buy your food from those farmers before you go to supermarkets. Is there any spirit you can relate to that you have felt on your own or that you know of thanks to the region's Indigenous People?

Connect

Just as you did with the tree, do the same with a nearby plant or flower, bowing to and/or prostrating yourself before it.

Question

Which birds live nearby or visit during their migration?

Connect

First thing in the morning, go to your door or window and listen to the birdsong. Don't start your day without doing this. If you can, learn about the type of food these birds prefer, and feed them regularly. How can you support their lives, their travels? Remember they need darkness when they migrate; turn off any exterior lights during that time. You can use both the rising and bowing gestures to relate to the birds. Is there any spirit you can relate to that you have felt on your own or that you know of thanks to the region's Indigenous People?

Question

What types of wild animals live in your area? Are their habits secure? Do you view them as a threat or as fellow creatures who have the right to life and their own ways of living? Why do wild animals show up in your backyard? Do they have enough space and resources to live, or are we invading their habitats? How can you protect both yourself and them?

Connect

When you see a living animal, do what you can to help it thrive. When you see the body of a dead animal, stop and say a prayer—even, perhaps, put on a pair of protective gloves and place the body under a tree, or some place where the earth can take it back up. Sing a song to the departed animal, and express your gratitude to it.

Question

If there is a river near your home, what is its name? What types of fish and other forms of life live in it? Is this body of water the main branch of a river or a tributary? How long has this river been here? Does it flow in a straight path or in a more serpentine fashion? Learn the differences. What is the river's present condition? How is it being used and for what purpose? Which companies are dumping toxins and garbage into the river? How does the city care for the river? How can you help protect and ensure that the river has a full life?

Connect

Go to the river and listen to the sounds of the water flowing. Pay attention to the vegetation growing along its banks; it can protect rivers from erosion. Learn about the fish and vegetation the river hosts, all the life it holds. Relate to the river through the gestures of bowing and prostrating. Is there any spirit you can relate to that you have felt on your own or that you know of thanks to the region's Indigenous People?

Question

Which phase is the moon currently in? What does each season bring to you and your area? What about the moon and seasons do you need to pay attention to?

Connect

Talk to the moon and salute its presence. Ask what it can tell you about how to live more in tune with the seasons. Use the gesture of rising to greet the moon.

Question

Is there any wind today? Where does it come from, and where is it going? What is the wind telling you?

Connect

Remember that there is a great Spirit living in your area. Perhaps you could connect to this spirit as the ruach of the Hebrew Scriptures or the Holy Spirit of the Christian tradition.

Question

High above the trees, just beyond the point of the atmosphere where all of our weather takes place, is the critical layer of the atmosphere where the highest concentration of ozone is found, protecting all life on earth. What is this place of wonder that keeps us alive?

Connect

As you raise your arms and body, be grateful for the ozone layer that allows us all to live.

Question

As you perform your gestures, what is beneath your feet? If it is topsoil, what makes this soil so rich? How can you protect all the little creatures and worms it contains? If you are standing on rocks, how old are they? What are they made of? What deep-time wisdom do they carry? If you are standing on cement, ask yourself why we need so much of it, allowing it to clog the earth's breathing. Can we uncover that patch of ground so that other plants and trees can live?

Connect

Prostrate yourself and touch the ground with your feet, knees, hands, or even your entire body. The movement of deep time is occurring beneath your feet, and so much life is in motion throughout the earth's crust. Try to learn who lives beneath your feet and how they live.

Question

What about your human neighbors? Who are they? What do they do? Where are they from? What are their stories and their struggles?

Connect

Turn to where your neighbors live and bow toward their homes. Say a prayer of well-being and kindness for them. Perhaps invite them over for coffee or offer something to honor them at the place you are doing the gesture.

Question

Of the people in your neighborhood, who is struggling? Does everyone have shelter? Are there clinics and hospitals for everyone? Is anyone going hungry? Are the children in your local schools able to eat three meals a day?

Connect

Rise up and ask for strength to engage in social, political, ecological, and religious gatherings aimed at finding collective ways of helping everyone who is struggling. Press the government to take responsibility for ensuring the well-being of everyone in the community.

Conclusion

For each act of connection, you can also find your own words to speak to each being. Words of gratitude, of sorrow, of longing, of desire, of need, of love, and so on. Within every gesture and throughout the movements taking place in your surroundings, from the ground below you to the skies above, deep medicine is doing its work—and you, small as your time and space may feel, are connecting to that healing movement in the vastness of planetary and universal time and space. Of course, we will not even come close with these questions to a comprehensive understanding of our relationship with the land—but we must begin, and begin now.

CHAPTER FIFTEEN

Why a Gesture? Why This Gesture?

To the skies I rise
To the earth I bow
To the ground I touch
In the earth I rest

That first gesture the Portuguese made in the new world—changing a tree from a living being worthy of life into a material good intended to serve human needs and desires—reveals how we first relate to the land as a commodity, not as an intrinsic part of who we are. Genocidal erasure of Indigenous Peoples as a means of possessing and exploiting land and forests is still rampant throughout the Americas, bringing with it the enslavement, exploitation, and commodification of the Black body. This religious worldview that made use of such tactics was grounded in patriarchy, white supremacy, hierarchies, anthropocentrism, the elevation of profit over sustainability, disconnection from the land, and development and growth as a cosmological norm intended to support our way of life. Out of one simple gesture, carried out casually by the colonizers, come the implications and complications, disorientation, and demands of a whole New World coming into being.

The bold intention of the three-gesture ritual I have described (rising, bowing, and prostrating) is to counter, symbolically and hopefully concretely, this ongoing colonial movement that continues to destroy the earth. This liturgical gesture offers a way to reimagine new forms of life by engaging on a micro level in spiritual, social, political, ecological, and economic forms of transformation. With the simple movements of rising, bowing, and prostrating, it is possible to envision and join other ways of caring for the earth by beginning new forms of relation and reconnection with the landscapes we live in.

These gestures are related to the three movements developed in my book *Inventory, Metamorphoses, and Emergenc(i)es*; in the ritual I discuss here, each gesture itself contains those three movements. Within each gesture is the taking of an *inventory*, meaning you must remember who and what came before you and what has happened to and in that place/space. It means remembering your responsibility of passing on that inventory and the place itself in as healthy a way as possible. Each gesture also features *metamorphosis*, which is an awareness of our current situation and the demands of our space/time. This awareness begs us to transform ourselves in order to meet the demands of this time and this space/place. Finally, within each gesture are *emergenc(i)es*: *emergencies,* meaning the need to pay attention to who and what is dying—people, animals, biomes, and everything within your environment—in order to lend assistance and aid what can hold onto life. And there are *emergences,* forms of life springing forth that must be tended, protected, and reciprocally engaged, diverse modes of being to which we must pay close attention.

Hence, within every gesture there is a concern with the past, excavating what has shaped our now; with the present, which demands continual change; and with the future, tending to what will emerge, in terms both of life and of destruction. It makes sense, then, to pause and understand where we are, where we have been, and where we'd like to be.

CHAPTER SIXTEEN

Decolonizing Ourselves

The Re(li)gion We Inhabit

The late Brazilian theologian Vitor Westhelle defined religion as "the excess present in the region: Re(li)gion," elaborating that "[t]he theological significance of the question of land and territory as 'absolute spaces' can be framed precisely in the juncture between the place that provides for the sustenance and reproduction of life, and the sentient space in which the spiritual dimension of existence, the excess we call the sacred, the space of the feast, can flourish."[116] If we are to take seriously, then, the notion of place/space and region, bioregion, we must attest to the fact that our spiritualities cannot depend solely on any transcendent being, be found in ourselves-as-discrete selves, or in the plethora of desires disentangled from the organic and material forces around us. Where our desires are concerned, spirituality has to do with a network of relations deeply related to the land we inhabit. We must learn that any spirituality has to be deeply entangled in a deep relation of body–spirit–territory, a conjunction of forces, that shapes and orients the land and us within a relationality of movement that spirals through the cyclical structure of time and place. Our individual physical lives rest within a much broader universe of life as a whole; it is within the complexities of many forms of life and reproduction and fullness of earthly beings that our life happens. We depend for our existence on our rootedness in and mutual belonging within a deeply entangled place, on our creation of festivities and celebrations, on the gift of being sustained by that bioregion, the ability of all beings of that place to live and be reproduced. Together, all of these things will foster cultivation/culture and a cultus/honor/worship fundamental to the existence of all the life-forms that inhabit that place.

These forms of dependence can be expressed by the Latin word *colere*, which takes on various meanings: to take care of, to cultivate, to till, to honor/worship. It also has the sense of inhabiting, nurturing, cherishing, and tending.[117] As Brazilian writer Alfredo Bosi says, "To take care of, the basic meaning of colo, not only implies attentiveness but also ordering."[118] This sense of the Latin verb describes practices of land keepers: caring for and ordering the land, following the law of the land. With time, the law and the lore of the land combine, and generating storylines and dreamtimes—oral stories and histories that transmit cosmological knowledge and ritual and cultural practices, and that ordain the spiritual relations between the human, more-than human, and natural worlds. The desires of a people are then oriented around those relations, where visible and invisible worlds are connected. Shamans, experts in those relations, provide guidance to the people.

Colonization, though, is the exact opposite of caring for, cultivating, honoring, attending to, and mostly, being led by the land. At the heart of the colonizing project is the uprooting of people from their land and all it contains—people, trees, vegetation, animals, mountains, rocks, water, and so much more—forcing them into another land for the sake of profit and power. When you uproot a person whose entire orientation toward life and belonging occurs thanks to and through the land, nothing is left intact for that person. Everything crumbles. And colonization is this very project of making everything crumble, an ongoing process of dis-placement, of removing us from place/space. In an uprooted society, the only things that remain are a sense of being a part of private places, the cultivation of money and particular ideas of success, the celebration of personal accomplishment, the honoring of placement within hierarchies, racial profiling, consumption as a form of belonging, financial hoarding as a form of sustenance, and the worship of foreign, out-of-place gods. This displacement has so altered our modes of being that we have lost our sense of time and placement.

On the other hand, it is necessary to also say that when we struggle to pay attention, we must also remember that capitalism leads us to excessive attention to many other things! We are bombarded with thousands of things demanding our attention every day, making us feel exhausted as we try to attend to what we think is necessary. In this battle, we tend to stay on the surface of things or the shortest spam of analysis and involvement. For example, we tend to reduce the necessary deep attention to the land to mere gestures without involvement; we combat ecological disasters with recycling only; self-care becomes self-help; and we understand people getting billionaires as long as they do philanthropy. In other words, the spirit of capitalism is so deep in us that it not only uproots us from the land and all its knowledge but turns our displacement into short forms of attention and easy ways of thinking, multiplying our desires in a way that we continue to be lost and disconnected from the land. Our displacement is such that it will take rounds and rounds of focusing our attention, and an ongoing dispossession of the spirit of capitalism. This can be done in different ways. What we are proposing here is the endless repetition of the gestures of this ritual to help us begin to pay attention to the land, saying no to our desires, and learn ways that will make us find our belonging to the land as we go beyond attention and begin composing our lives with the many worlds of other beings who exist with us within our bioregion.

Every time we pay attention to something, we are also not paying attention to something else. A couple of examples. When we pay attention to the bees only, we may lose attention to the pesticides that poison the land, the lack of fresh water for the plants, the lack of diversity of plants, the necessary habitat for other animals, and to weeds that can be important presences in the bioregion. Also, as we wrestle with our religious formations, we must be alerted to our own monotheistic leanings toward a transcendent being, which can also be translated in a secular form of nature as a single being. If we focus on transcendence, we may continue valuing life on earth in hierarchical structures oriented by the spirit of capitalism. We will also lose the full immanence/transcendence of all beings who are present around us, with all their gifts, carrying the fullness of life in themselves, composing differently with the earth in ways that organize the full conditions of our common living. Thus, depending on who or what we are paying attention to, it can produce a counter-effect, that is, a growing lack of belonging to the earth while thinking that we are relating to the land.

Moreover, attention has also to do with time and our understanding and engagement with it. There is a difference between a pre- and a supposed post-modernity in relation to time, and it has to do with the speed with which we live our lives, a dramatic change of pace that has emerged over a mere 500 years, and which has been vastly enabled and accelerated by multiple forms of technology. When the Portuguese first landed in Brazil, it would have taken one person quite a bit of time to fell a tree; today, machines can take down hundreds of trees in seconds. Over the course of twelve months of Jair Bolsonaro's presidency, 1 billion trees—thirty-two trees per second—were cut down in the Amazon.[119]

The colonial enterprise and its embrace of placelessness has profoundly influenced the ways we relate to each other and to the land. Aimé Césaire, a poet, author, and politician from Martinique, demands that we

> admit once and for all, without flinching at the consequences, that the decisive actors here are the adventurer and the pirate, the wholesale grocer and the ship owner, the gold digger and the merchant, appetite and force, and behind them, the baleful projected shadow of a form of civilization which, at a certain point in its history, finds itself obliged, for internal reasons, to extend to a world scale the competition of its antagonistic economies.[120]

These actors are still with us, though they go by different names. The pirates, the wholesale grocers, and the ship owners, the gold diggers and the merchants of our times are the organizers of the market; the publicists and fake news makers; so many politicians, the financial brokers; the CEOs of fossil fuel ventures, of mining, logging, and fishing companies. Everyone, that is, who allows colonial capitalism to continue uprooting our world, puts us in competition, insulates us with greed, and encourages us to devour the earth and ourselves. A single tree was used for that first cross; now, an entire mountain is mined to produce energy for private jets and opulent forms of living for the rich, clean waters are exhausted to run artificial intelligence, soil is ransacked for gold—the list goes on. Modernity has brought with it an increased colonial appetite and forces that threaten to devour everything in sight. The spirit of capitalism demands a fast pace which is suicidal and is indeed killing us all!

Over five hundred years' worth of uprootedness and constant disconnection from space and place has entailed the loss and death of an entire web of relations characterized by deep interdependence with the land. Almost everything we do these days is disconnected from the earth, including the pace of the earth. What modernity did was to impose artificial times unrelated to the earth. Hardly any of the rituals meant to shape our lives—myths, stories, rites of passage, feasts, celebrations, and other forms of relations and belonging—connect us with the time of the earth. For many, spirituality or religion has very little to do with, or engages very rarely with space-time or place-time. Rituals are mostly related to the inside of worship sites and temples.

In many ways, Hegel's maxim "the truth of space is time" has become the mark of our uprootedness from the land.[121] When monotheistic religions imposed on us a universal God, our relationships with the local gods who were deeply connected with the land were contested, demonized, and finally erased. The God of transcendence destabilized the spatial notion of the sacred, and immanence was subjected to volatile and confused theological assumptions.

With the entrance of the colonizing project into the world, that tendency only continued to develop and gain strength, to the point that we now live exclusively in time, linear time to be more precise, and not in space/place. Influenced by the work of Anthony Giddens, Westhelle says that "[t]he result [of this uprooting] is that space is perceived as a homogeneous infrastructure over which—instead of in and through which—events take place."[122] Unsurprisingly, a large portion of theological discourse is nothing more than a placeless monologue wrapped up in time, a one-track spaceless sermon that pays no heed to Indigenous theologies or the plight of Palestine. To be able to consider people and places outside of its conversation, theology would have to land, would have to face the theft and destruction of territory, which is itself fundamentally about the destitution and the destruction of people.

If we take the Christian liturgy, for instance, we find a homogenous project of time, of temporalization of space. In liturgical theology, space is an undeveloped concept and time content, flow, and development to a placeless message. Christians turned the Jewish connection with the land and the relationships it entailed into a temporal celebration. For example, the Jewish festival of Pentecost involved offering the first fruits brought in from the harvest—but when Christians adopted it, Pentecost turned into a celebration of the arrival and presence of the Holy Spirit. A festival grounded in the material world began to understand the material involved as a variety of spoken tongues. From that point on, the relationship with the first fruits—the land— and the complexities of living languages in place, was lost.

Moreover, if we look at the Christian feast of Advent, we realize this remembrance is about Jesus's arrival within a particular territory experiencing a number of conflicts unique to it—including the fact that Jesus's parents had to flee so that their son wouldn't be killed. Today, Advent has lost all its political and geographical markers of tension and has become no more than an unmarked time at the end of the year to mark the birth of Jesus with only thoughts of placeless hope, peace, joy, and love. Time within time: a date set aside for our attention without the experience of place and conflict. That nonsituated notion of time also means the believer fails to consider the time of celebration in relation to place. That is why the genocide in Palestine is not an issue for many Christians whose Jesus is mostly a product of an unmarked time and placeless belief.

The liturgical calendar is based on the life of Jesus and has very little to do with the seasons of the year, the stages of the moon and the circulations and flow of the oceans, the movements of the wind, the regulations of the soil, the migrations of species, the transitions of different seasons in various bioregions, the kinds of foods available to each time, the limits and gifts of every season.

Mostly, Christianity has become a religion of time, in which spirituality has no place to land. As historian of religion Jonathan Z. Smith says, "Temporality became the means to overcome topography."[123] In contrast to Jesuit priest and scholar Michel de Certeau's assertion that "[p]lace is practiced space"[124]—which I interpret here to mean that the laws according to which the natural world functions preexist us and demand we act in accordance with them, even as those laws adapt and change to new circumstances—Christianity never actually understood itself as existing within or responding to a particular place, instead continuing on its way according to its own unchanging script. This script of placelessness, or banishment of (the importance of) place, propelled Christianity to colonize, to conquer, destroy, and uproot.

It also transformed spirituality into the stuff of a spirit living within (usually eschatological) time, always in an elsewhere. For Christian spirituality, which feared and continues to fear pagan rootedness, place and time do not exist together. Wrapped in the promise of an eternal future elsewhere, aligned with Jesus's own declaration that we are not of this world,[125] it has become unnecessary for Christians to engage with space, which is itself nothing of theological, spiritual, or liturgical concern. In fact, some forms of Christian eschatology claim that the worse the world becomes, the closer Jesus is to returning and taking us to the place that really matters: heaven. To be with Jesus in heaven is the apex of some forms of Christian spiritual life.

One way out of placeless thoughts for thinkers of all sorts, especially religious thinkers, is to familiarize themselves with Indigenous Knowledge. Indigenous Knowledge is often place-based and it can help us reorient time to place. Eduardo Viveiros de Castro reminds us of this need when he analyzes the work of Davi Kopenawa:

> Davi Kopenawa helps us put the famous "ideas out of place" in their proper place, because his is a discourse about place, and because its enunciator knows what his place is, where it is, and what it is. It is time, then, to confront ourselves with the ideas of this place that we have taken from the indigenous peoples with fire and sword, and declared "ours" without the slightest shame; ideas that constitute, above all, a global theory of place, generated locally by the indigenous peoples, in the concrete and etymological sense of the latter word.[126]

Time is fundamentally correlated to space. When something is to happen in time, it also means it is happening in a space. Tyson Yunkaporta says that time is not a discrete entity, but a relational one. To put things in the right relation, time and space must be related. He admonishes us to put space and time together. He also says that perhaps, we should change the language, and use hyphenated words like "place-time," "time-place," which mean

> a seasonal moment in a particular regional location… Because it kind of demands of people, if you are asking them what time something happens, it demands that people are thinking about the place where they are and what's gonna be going on there. ... Time doesn't account for all your relations with humans and nonhumans, and the seasons… in time-place, place as meaning, place is specific, seasonally and regionally in a million ways, it has story, it has meaning in all these spatial places, your maps of meaning on it, your travel roots and what they mean to you and how you store your knowledge in that, every human being has that.[127]

But we don't think in that way. If we think about Christianity, its God is a God out of place, who lives everywhere and nowhere—in no particular place. Heaven, in this regard, is a place without a place. Theological and spiritual discourses and practices often have nothing to say about the land, perhaps fearing that doing so will turn Christianity into a form of paganism. This placelessness of spirituality, which we can say is also an ontological displacement, became even more pronounced with colonialism's uprooting project, which encouraged the church to continue its relation with the land as an empire, to move into capitalizing and privatizing the land. It was an ongoing movement of controlling, domination, and stealing of the land from Indigenous Peoples. The colonizing conquest used the Holy Spirit as the guiding force to objectify the land and the people of the land. Neither the people of the land, nor the land itself, had "soul" in them; thus both were only objects of conquest.

Both colonialism and Christianity have uprooted cultures materially and spiritually. Not only do we not know where we belong, there is in fact nowhere to belong. Our belonging lies in an identity without a land, a name without a territory, a religion without place. Acting to change that reality, the three-gesture religious ritual I describe here aims to reground us in the earth, a *religare* to the land. This ritual is also intended to open our senses to a larger sense of spirituality and to bring us to an understanding that spiritualities are fundamental to any form of individual/collective forms of healing in our relationship with the land. Its purpose, in other words, is to reveal religion as being part of a territory, and spirituality as related to a bioregion. As described in the introduction, a simultaneously local and universal movement.

The critique begets a way forward. A much fuller sense of life than the one presented by colonial Christianity is offered by Indigenous paradigms that deeply connect bodies, territories, and worlds: bodies are related to territories; individuals can only exist within a collective. In this way, the notion of "us" again, includes people *and* all other forms of life: animals, vegetation, minerals, and waters, living together in relationality and reciprocity. Together, we sustain the ongoing circle of life: in stories, myths, and spirits, myriad life-forms converge upon and within this wondrous being we call earth. But the notion of we/us is complex and filled with knots and weaving threads. The we without hierarchies, without us knowing precisely the other, our boundaries, our limits, and possibilities. Every time a *we* is uttered in this text, it has to be understood as a bundle of specific presences, of agencies, places, spirit/Spirit/s, connections, oppositions, antagonisms, relations, divergences, and so on. In the *we* lives the they, an I in multiple relations that connects, repulses, entangles, and escapes. The we are always affecting and being affected in constant motions in different times and spaces.

Anthropologist Maria De la Cadena also offers an ample definition of "we":

> My conceptual and political wager is for a complex "we" composed of an "us" and a "them" occupying (and being) in a partially connected time-place while at the same time exhibiting not difference but divergence, that is, what makes each (of "us" and "them") be. This "complex we" implodes the possibility of a single locus of enunciation of the "self" because "us" and "them" occupy it, always considering that even in divergence "we" affect each other. Unlike the simple we, the "complex we" is with what exceeds what the usual "we" is not... This "complex we"

> is a shared condition from which "self" and "other" emerge relationally as intra-acted assertions of divergence.[128]

This we has to be thought through the colonizing forces of hierarchies, subordination, and homogenization, of race construction, of the distinction between poverty/savage/nature and richness/civilization/society, of the abstraction of bios without geos, time without space, human without other species. But more than that, there is that which we cannot see, feel, or ordain in our very notion of we. In the complex we of Cadena, there are always the excesses of humans and animals and spirit/Spirit/s. It is what she calls the *anthropo-not-seen,* which gives us indeed a very complex way to start thinking about the *we*. This citation is lengthy but, it is very helpful in understanding the *we* we are talking about:

> A neologism intended as a counterpart to the Anthropocene, it signals the world-making process whereby worlds that do not make themselves through practices that separate ontologically humans (or culture) from nonhumans (or nature)—nor necessarily conceive as such the different entities in their assemblages—are both obliged into that distinction and exceed it. The anthropo-not-seen thus refers to both the will (and the world) that obliges the distinction (and destroys what disobeys the obligation) and the excesses to that will: the collectives that are composed with entities that are not only human or nonhuman because they are also with what (according to the obligation) they should not be—humans with nonhumans (and vice versa.) The anthropo-not-seen mentions existents that are within a historically formulated hegemonic condition of impossibility: they simply cannot be—therefore they are not-seen, not-heard, not-felt, not-known. Importantly, they exceed radical conceptualizations like that of the human as more than human, or the history of human nature as the history of interspecies relationship: neither geos or bios, the anthropo-not-seen that is all entities that are through relations that cannot be (to return to my previous example, the hunter through the elk he not not-is) may be dangerously denied being (or benevolently ignored as unimportant) if their possibility is not considered in a "complex we" grounded in divergence (rather than in sameness.) Instead, if replete with monsters—those that cannot be—the "complex we" has the potential both to challenge the destructive imposition of sameness performed by the world that founded the anthropos and to be unafraid of the unknown that their emergence may inaugurate.[129]

That very notion of the anthropo-not-seen is fundamental to the very notion of Re(li)gion mentioned above from Vitor Westhelle which defines religion as "the excess present in the region: Re(li)gion." That is to say that through these gestures, we are dealing with what we cannot know fully, a kind of natural and supernatural combination of many "wes" we are in relation and contact with when we rise, bow or prostrate to any other living being near us.

However, that does not mean we should stop doing the ritual gestures but to perform them with deep caution. We continue with the challenge to listen to the earth, and adopt a form of spirituality centered in the land and all living things, sacra-mentalities, response-abilities to the ways of the earth, a way of world-making care, a full body/spirit connection with the land.[130] Even other religions will have to engage a plethora of enunciations, consider their bioregions and engage in this re(li)gious spirituality somehow, somewhat! There is a need to reinvent our spiritualities in the heart of the earth, for only a place, a region, a land, and its spirit/Spirit/s can sustain us and keep us alive.

For example, in the case of Christianity, when one brings the fullness of Eucharistic bread to what is called the word of God,[131] one has to think of bread in terms of the wheat, the soil, the water and seeds, the sun, the climate, farming, the whole bioregion, the workers involved, their wages, distribution, hunger, notions of ownership, and so much more. Combining bread with the word of God, or the Spirit in place, would result in a full re(li)gion, where the bounty of the region that provides the bread is the very excess present in that place, an excess we could call the Spirit. That is the re(li)gion we need! As Westhelle says, "The maintenance of the spiritual significance of the geographical experience of a group is precisely what warrants rootedness, whether fixed or mobile."[132] Here, Christianity would be closer to what professor of religion Mark Wallace calls *Christianimism*, where "[h]ealthy interactions with nature are resonant with the 'incantatory gesture' characteristic of Christian animism: summoning the presence of the numinous within the everyday."[133]

If we thought about re(li)gion as deeply attached to a place, to a biore(li) gion, then rituals would actually make sense—because at their core, rituals help things, people, and structures to exist, to emerge and grow and change, to prosper and endure *within a particular place*. And for rituals to take place, we must attend to and focus on that particular place-time. Smith makes plain that "ritual is, first and foremost, a mode of paying attention. It is a process for marking interest."[134] A process, in other words, for taking place. The notion of the sacred is then located in the place we pay attention, in the excess of life flowing out of that space.[135] Contemporary ritual theorist and practitioner Ronald Grimes adds complexity to Smith's assertion; according to him, rituals bring together all the complexities of the geographical, the social, the historical, the political, and the biological.[136] Through rituals, then, we drench ourselves in the living and dying of a particular biore(li) gion, so that we can find the spirit/Spirit/s of the place: re(li)gion!

FIGURE 5 *The common ground of life.*

CHAPTER SEVENTEEN

Rituals

Bodies–Territories–Worlds

As a spiritual action of remembrance, awareness, and connection, this liturgical gesture aims to enact, in a simple yet complex way, the correlation between bodies, territories, and worlds. Our bodies can only be known in relation to the territory we live in; our territory can only be explained by the bodies and the many worlds that live in it; and the many worlds we share in our territories mark the presence of so many bodies inhabiting so many forms of life within these territories. These bodies–territories–worlds compose and are composed of spirits, stories, presences, ghosts, cosmologies, forms of living, and the ancestral wisdom of the earth. Every ritual gesture must pay attention to these presences.

The notion of body–territory comes from Indigenous Brazilian women, who know that to defend their territories is to defend their bodies and the bodies of their people. Sonia Guajajara, now Brazil's Minister of Indigenous Peoples, has defined the notions of territory and bodies:

> The territory is what guarantees our life. Our body is what is at stake, it is what is being targeted by violence. And the spirit is our identity, our connection with our ancestry that guarantees the strength of our culture to continue resisting. And these issues are related because when men invade our territories, they directly affect our bodies and our identity.[137]

Because the relationship between bodies and territories orients the world in which Indigenous women live, I add the word "world" to this two-term notion. Here, the concept "world" points to the fact that in every body–territory lives many worlds, worlds of spirits, of ancestors, of many species, of people–people, people–trees, people–birds, people–plants, people–rivers, and so on.

In 2019, Brazil's National Forum of Indigenous Women led the inaugural Indigenous Women's March. Under the motto "Territory: Our Body, Our Spirit," they highlighted the notion of spirit as intrinsic to their bodies–territories and worlds, as *living* in their territories and their bodies. Without the presence of the spirit(s), neither they nor their people could exist. The kinship relations that orient their daily lives and expansive cosmologies include a living relationship with the spirit(s).

This lived understanding is related to what philosopher Donna Haraway calls situated knowledge, which requires thinking with the "apparatus of bodily production." Here, bodies are "material-semiotic generative nodes. Their boundaries materialize in social interaction."[138] This knowledge tells us that in order to confront the current climate crisis with any form of hope, we must profoundly reorient ourselves within and to the world. And that requires reconsidering the relationship between our bodies, territories, and worlds. But what does that mean?

It means first of all to recognize that our bodies are *not* discrete, autonomous entities—that is, we need to dispel the illusion that we are enough for ourselves, that each individual can make it on their own. On the contrary! We can only live in a relationship, not only with other human bodies but also with other bodies that compose our territories: vegetation, rivers, topsoil, insects, animals, rocks, and so on. Each of these actors are worlds in themselves—and so our territories, the neighborhoods we live in, are themselves filled with many different and complex worlds. Not only schools, offices, churches, and the downtown area, but the whole geography and ecology of the place, with its parks, rivers, trees, birds, flowers, vegetation, rural areas, climate, and entire landscape that compose our bodies–territories–worlds. We actually *are* this complex space, and unless our whole being undergoes a metamorphosis, no real transformation will take place.

How do we begin this grand transformation? With rituals. The people who inhabit bodies–territories–worlds know them very well. What I am calling ritual is related to what Indigenous scholar Vine Deloria Jr. calls ceremony, "the ceremonies that constitute the spiritual life of the tribal community."[139] For Indigenous Peoples, ceremonies contain within them ancestral knowledge-practice that makes them who they are. Every ceremony has to do, in some way or another, with bodies–territories–worlds: stories, spirits, awareness, forms of relating to the land, means of reaching resolution, ways of calling upon presences or for protection, songs, artifacts, and more. Ceremonies are performances of all known and unknown forms of life; they carry on and pass along knowledge, ways of being and feeling and relating to new generations. As Deloria says, "The Indian community passes knowledge along over the generations as a common heritage that is enriched by the experiences of both individuals and groups of people in the ceremonies. Both the ceremony and the people's interpretation of it change as new insights are gained."[140]

Ceremonies retain the wisdom of the land. And as the fundamental forms of knowing and practices of a people, they have also proven to be one of the most powerful ways Indigenous Peoples of the Americas have survived over 500 years of colonization and genocide.

Sadly, Western civilization's tendency to compartmentalize every aspect of life means that ritual has been detached from knowledge. The wisdom of entire spirit-territories has been turned into a topic for *scholarship*, a form of knowing acquired by reading books.

Some scholars, though—especially ritual theorists—have overcome this tendency, trying to pull us away from this disembodied understanding. They want to expand the notion of ritual, understanding it as a performance that keeps, creates, and leads to the evolution of worlds; a performance that orients the way we live. Ronald Grimes tells us that "[i]n ritualizing, human beings discover, then embody and cultivate their world views, attitudes, and ethics."[141] Rituals, then, must have a central place in our spiritualities—that is, our forms of perception and living.

In 2003, more than twenty years before the concept of climate disaster, much less those of fossil fuel and extractionist capitalism, had become widespread, Grimes described ritual's importance in confronting ecological catastrophe:

> Few people consider rites an effective means for saving the planet from environmental destruction. Ask the ordinary person, "Should we expect anything of environmental significance from ritual or performance?" and the reply will probably be, "No. Why would anyone even raise such a question?" Yet we are witnessing the emergence of groups and individuals who consider it obvious that ritual is one, if not the, answer to the environmental conundrum. They consider it urgent that humans learn, or re-learn, ritual ways of becoming attuned to their environments.[142]

I count myself among those who *consider it urgent that humans learn, or re-learn, ritual ways of becoming attuned to their environments.* But for that (re)learning to happen, we must undergo a change of sense and sensibility, of ways of believing and participating, thinking and feeling, before we can recreate worlds as places where it is possible to live and survive. The words of Portuguese poet Fernando Pessoa—"What feels in me is thinking"—provide an entry into an expansive spirituality, one that feels-thinks in relationship with the land, with the worlds of all other beings around us, each containing a specific perspective.[143] This radical relational spirituality engenders collective forms of living in response-ability, reciprocity, and gratitude throughout and within the territory in which we all stand.

This type of spirituality is related to what French poet Paul Valéry calls sensitivity, a "faculty," he says,

> which is fundamental and which is wrongly opposed to intelligence, of which it is, on the contrary, the true driving force. I am speaking of sensitivity. If the sensitivity of modern man [*sic*] is strongly compromised by the current conditions of his life, and if the future seems to promise this sensitivity an increasingly severe treatment, we have the right to believe that intelligence will suffer profoundly from the alteration of sensitivity.[144]

Today, our sensitivity, or driving force, is at the mercy of capitalism. The only way to break this force and build bodies–territories–worlds is by constructing a new sensibility, a new intelligence, tapping on a new driving force capable of evoking feelings, modes of thinking, and practices that are opposed to those in capitalism's thrall. While various practices are needed, I focus here on rituals, or on ritualizing new forms of life, found at the heart of these changes.

Grimes has pushed us to think about many forms of *ritualizing*, of creating rituals appropriate for our time and place. Rituals keep us alive and moving through times and spaces, and they continue to make sense of the ways we live. As he says, rituals "are not supposed to reflect culture, rather they are supposed to account for it, or lay the grounds for its evaluating."[145]

Reflecting culture might mean the continuation of practices and assumptions that uphold detachment, dissociation, and exclusion, hindering transformation. In the same way, rituals that only reflect unchanging theological beliefs can be dangerous, for they can act as revolving doors, things-in-themselves, enacted in order to preserve and perpetuate a certain religion rather than to allow for and encourage transformation required for our survival. On the other hand, in ritualizing new ways of living, we must be careful not to jump on the bandwagon of sheer newness, but must instead investigate various sources of wisdom and amplify what they have given us. Religions have managed to preserve wisdom throughout their changing histories, and ritualization is the process of keeping these traditions alive by ensuring that they meet our current needs and expanding their possibilities.

Musician and composer Jon Batiste may help to fill out what's happening here. He describes his album *Beethoven Blues*, a new reading of Beethoven with his New Orleans heart, as

> being in conversation with Beethoven and extending his music.... Take Beethoven's music and exist within the music as if you were co-composing with him and adding all the elements that... existed after his time on earth. So you have things like flamenco music or gospel music, soul music, jazz music, and blues primarily, which to me is the, not just musical innovation of the twentieth century, but an innovation of human expression and spirituality.... It's the opportunity of a lifetime for an artist, and the blues provides that.[146]

Batiste deeply reveres Beethoven. In thoroughly learning to play the composer's music, he came to love it—and in reading that music along with the blues, he is making Beethoven available to people who wouldn't have known his work otherwise. Batiste is traditioning Beethoven; bringing his genius into the contemporary world with a twist expands the composer's reach even further. The conversation between the two musicians arrives at a point where neither classical music nor blues serves as a platform for the other; instead, each becomes something new, unique, and each is transformed.

In a similar way, ritualization is the traditioning of religions toward the transformation of culture, of economics, of politics, of life in fullness. As Batiste says about the expansiveness of music, "At the end, it is not about music, it is about life." As we craft new rituals, then, we must also evaluate what about them works, what needs to be revised, what needs to be expanded, what needs to be discontinued, and so on. Evaluation is a dynamic process, requiring refashioning along with life and reality as they fluctuate. Where rituals and theories are concerned, everything shifts continuously: "Theories and definitions change, usually in patterns consonant with changed cultural practices."[147] We must ensure that our cultural practices do not lag behind.

The ritualizing process is what will get us through the unknowns, through fearful times. Rituals make us aware of who we are and who we must become alongside the land we inhabit. We must give our bodies–territories–worlds over to ritualization in order to gain new forms of awareness, new means of commitment, new forms of politics, new actions and practices, new ways of relating to territories and their spirit/Spirit/s, new work habits, all while understanding our landscape as a core part of our being. Rituals will allow us to intertwine our subjectivities with the subjectivities of other species, developing senses and spiritualities that will engage ways of living never considered before.

> But again, what are rituals, exactly? Let's look once more at what Grimes has to say:
> More important than a definition of ritual is a sense for it.
> Ritual is nothing if not a sensuous activity.
> A sense of ritual arises from participation in rituals that activate the senses.
> You don't have to define the word automobile to drive one.
> You don't have to define the word computer to use a word processor.
> You don't define ritual any more than lovers define love.
> You define words, "ritual" and "love," or use images.
> The quotation marks remind you to exercise humility,
> to remember that you are not defining reality.
> You are defining words.
> Maybe you know people who cook or garden

by actions rather than by recipe or guidebook.
Even though they may, or may not,
be able to explain what they do,
they do a fabulous job
because they have a sense for it.
"How much baking powder?" I once asked my grandmother.
Her reply was tossed off predictably, "You know, just enough."
"Where do hollyhocks grow best?" I asked her.
"Oh, you know, wherever it seems right."
The craving for how-to manuals
attests to the lack of a sense for ritual.
If you have a sense for something,
you don't need books.
What you need most can't be provided by books.
The problem with do-it-yourself manuals
is that they can't cultivate a sense for a ritual,
a felt, embodied knowledge that enables you to act
constructively in situations calling for a ritual response.[148]

Grimes's understanding has emerged out of his deep engagement and wrestling with practices and theories from across the globe—where his thinking has been shaped by actually performing rituals himself. I will never forget the advice he offered when, fresh out of school and new to my first teaching position, I asked him what I should be reading with students. I have held onto his answer ever since: "Take your students to the chapel, have them walk around, feel the space, know who is there. Is this space a he, she, it? What is the story of this chapel, what can they see? When you do rituals, open the doors and let the fragrance of the flowers and the fresh and new foliage of the season enter the space with its aromas and walk around with that smell. Then have them sleep there. Start a relationship with that space."

The three-part ritual offered in this book comes from this sort of spiritual thinking-feeling-practice, and is intended to be a spiritual resource for our times that can be thought–felt–practiced individually and collectively. It makes use of open-ended forms of practice and theoretical reasoning so that readers can take it anywhere, change it according to their needs and environment, move it, draw upon it as they care for the land, and grow into the land's ways of living and surviving.

This ritual is rooted in the profound trust that by practicing it, something latent within us will see the light of day. The performance of these gestures is nothing other than the birth of larger commitments to lands and rivers, animals and entire landscapes, new forms of politics, new radical expressions of protest; of the ability to see each patch of land blooming with spirit/Spirit/s who live with and protect every sentient being around us.

Common people possess agency; they can do the work of the spirit/Spirit/s and tap into their collective creativity; they can activate cultural, political, economic, and ecological interventions; they can stop movements of death and provide access to webs of life, for themselves and for the generations who come after them. I believe that rituals can activate change in ourselves and in our worlds—not only among humans but also with countless other beings who can in fact teach us how to ritualize our lives. If we can mimic the lives of the bees, the ants, the birds, the waters, or the soil, we can ritualize a life that is in sync with our surroundings and discover a life so rich and new that we might even lose our desire for the synthetic things we keep accumulating.

Only when these rituals inscribe new cosmologies into our very bones can we learn to orient ourselves using the movement of the sun and moon, ancestral knowledge of stars and universes. When we place our tiny selves into the hands of our present earth and the flow of immemorial time, our now is suffused with fullness and wonder. And if our rituals demand that we become responsible for our bodies–territories–worlds, we cannot *but* redesign the ways in which we produce everything we have come to depend on, from the operation of machines and factories to the ways we plant and grow food. We will be forced to transform the ways we eat, live, work, play, and love.

Grimes reminds us that rituals can help reorient our cosmologies, and that cosmologies can also set limits upon our rituals:

> Cosmologies are as important for what they tell ritualists not to perform as for what they tell them to perform. In the middle-of-the-road world many of us inhabit, we are not ritually supposed to sweat, stay up all night, sleep in the sanctum, enter trance, or let wild sounds escape the throat. All rites, even the holiest of liturgies, express time-bound values and space-bound peculiarities. They are suffused by the same spiritual and intellectual pollution that we all breathe in order to stay alive. So neither ritual theories nor ritual systems are free of the obligation to serve the ground we walk on, the water we drink, the air we breathe. Like Rappaport, I am speaking about what rites ought or might do. We will not know what ecologically attuned rites actually do apart from ritual experiment and critique. To wait, hoping for certainty before acting, is a greater risk than hoping to learn by acting.[149]

Spirit-filled ritual, then, can be this "learn by acting" form of living, acting like a compass, guiding us as we go, reorienting our practices, our education, our prayers, our neighborhoods. And then we will take on the destroyers of our world and say no more—no more!

In a nutshell, this book offers a spiritual practice, a spiritual method, a way of thinking–feeling–doing as being in a world that is vanishing before our eyes. I do hesitate to use the phrase "spiritual practices" because of the many awful, almost irredeemable ways it gets used. I haven't, though, found any other way to describe what I believe lies at the heart of what we must do in the world as it is now—that is, discover and create ritual practices capable of enacting new ways of living, postponing the end of the world. Ritual practices centered on our bodies–territories–worlds that welcome and engage with new stories, new relations, new theologies, new desires, ancient knowledge, and necessary new forms of living.

CHAPTER EIGHTEEN

Fetishes, Prayers, and Spiritualities

It's not hard to sense that we are living in the midst of huge crises—social, economic, political, ecological, epistemological, and so many more—all of which point to the spiritual source of our collective bankruptcy. The spirit of capitalism has swallowed our spirit and the spirit of the land, and has turned everything into a fetish with surplus value! A fetish is a spell, a thing that has no spirit of its own, but is turned into some new thing when it receives a spirit, a value, a magical power. Capitalism's power disassociates us from the natural world and replaces our prior connection within a larger web of belonging. Disconnected, we are trapped in a new web of false needs that the spell of capitalism would have us believe are essential for survival.

We were reoriented toward mass consumption and identities based on what we own and aim to own. Capitalism and many forms of religion situate human beings outside our organic chains of relationships and webs of correspondences, turning us into consumerist Frankensteins, assemblages of spare parts that must keep working in order to keep the engine of consumption going. With our psyches and subjectivities already shaped by the fetishism of the market, we live under a spell/spirit that has nothing to do with the spirit/Spirit/s of the land. The spirit/Spirit/s of our time has cut us off from any relationship with the land, and paces our lives according to the speed at which our endless, fetishized commodities are produced and purchased. Our desires have been kidnapped, our *joie de vivre* turned into anxiety, our sense of self deformed into it-self; it is very hard to see ourselves as parts of a whole, a complement and fundamentally related to other beings. Instead, we have become mirrors unto ourselves, handed therapies that try to help us with behaviorist responses and/or understand ourselves by going "deep within."

What we call spiritualities have also been kidnapped and fetishized, made to run at the market's pace, grown weak, and undisciplined. Half of our soul runs amok like a headless chicken trying to survive, feeling anxious and unwell, aiming at something only vaguely grasped, while the other half tries to seize upon any so-called spiritual practice that can offer a quick fix. Our spiritualities have also turned into a mimicry of the other; we mimic each other's habits of buying, dressing, and living.[150] This repetition of the same alludes to a swirling condition where desire desires desire, and desire exists as the endless names and products that vanish as soon as one owns it. Our spiritualities are our desiring subjectivities, all owned by capitalism. As Ernest Dichter said, "Human desire is the raw material we are working with. The strategy of human desire is the tool of shaping the human factor, the most important aspect of our worldly arsenal."[151]

The fetishization of Christian religious faiths has either turned the core of religion into a hierarchical structure where high priests wear long robes, golden rings, pointy hats, ancient symbols, and golden liturgical artifacts, or has eviscerated itself of every symbol, all substance, or particular historical content. Rich, complex religious practices have been turned into coaching, lessons in achieving prosperity that requires invasion of other countries and the establishment of despotic, dictatorial religions. While coaching has become the individualized religion of our day, making the individual the center of social life, the prosperity gospel has turned a fundamentally collective form of life into celebration of personal gain and accomplishment, while religious nationalism turns religious commitment into political domination. Following the Spirit of capitalism, these individualized and socialized understandings of the religious and spiritual have provided new ways to orient extreme right politics, fascism, and the consolidation of empire.

Contemporary spirituality is inhabited by the power of the fetish, where the animating spirit is committed to continued disassociation and conquest that pushes us to strive for social status at the expense of the land's call for reconnection. I may be talking about spirituality as metaphysics in Italian philosopher Giambattista Vico's sense:

> as rational metaphysics teaches that man becomes all things by understanding them, this imaginative metaphysics shows that man becomes all things by not understanding them; and perhaps the latter proposition is truer than the former, for when man understands he extends his mind and takes in the things, but when he does not understand he makes the things out of himself and becomes them by transforming himself into them.[152]

In other words, the spirit that guides and shapes our lives and our spiritualities is so confused that it has driven us to create the things that surround us in our own image—and then to turn around and try to transform ourselves into the very things we have created. Thus, our spirit is one of inanimate things that exist in submission to our development and acquisition. It is the spirituality of a fetish, one that orients our perceptions and sensibilities, is prey to emotions of greed and fear, is always pressed into forms of self-development, always conquering and keeping up with the busy world, continually pushing us for more and more to a supposed greatness! The spirituality of the fetish is both symptom and cause of our exhausted and exhausting capitalistic spiritual selves. And any exhausted spirituality can only produce confusion and death.

The spirit of fetish is one of destruction, violence, and death. Jesus's words could have easily described that spirit, born of colonialism and capitalism—the spirit of the thief: "The thief comes only to steal and kill and destroy."[153] Apply that observation to the spirit of fetish, and an entirely new way of knowing, of being, of perception becomes apparent. It is in fact a new Spirit: of colonization and capitalism, apotheosis of the fetish! This spirit steals everything from us: our relationship with the land, with each other, with ourselves. This spirit steals our health and makes us sick. This spirit throws off balance the energies of our world.

We are reaching an end, though, of this spirit's force; we have reached a point where the earth can no longer provide what we want to extract from it. We are borrowing from future generations, and even the "funds" to make that borrowing possible are being depleted. In some parts of the world, we have already surpassed the 1.5-degree Celsius increase in global temperature that scientists have long warned us would lead to catastrophic changes.[154] We are at a crossroads: we either let the spirit of fetish—the spirit of disaster, panic, and catastrophe—continue to lead us, or we face up to the crises it causes and inaugurate a spiritual revolution able to establish global forms of care, reciprocity, and transformation. If we don't stop the spirit of fetish, the earth will—because this spirit of the thief has no relation to the spirit/Spirit/s that orient the earth.

This spirit of fetish is grounded in two-faced symbols of domination such as money and possessions—that convince us, in other words, that we are the dominators, while also and actually dominating us. Thinking of land as our possession provides us with a sense of control and dominium, of ownership of the objects and subjects found within and upon it—and all the while we fail to realize that we are in fact controlled by that land. And money is a spiritual symbol that orients us. It shapes our subjectivity and controls our sovereignty, while making us think that it allows us to control the world's subjectivity (actually treating the world as an object) and achieve (i.e., buy!) sovereignty of self—over other humans and every other form of life: nations and states, animals, vegetation, waters, mountains, even time, and space. Money and property never exist in isolation, and are much more than neutral means of exchange; they are spiritual symbols fetishized by the capitalist spirit. The ways our lives are organized—socially, politically, culturally, and more—are structured by this spirituality acting through the religious symbols of capitalism.

Hence, we need a different spirituality, one detached, as much as possible, from the all-pervasive, all-fetishizing spirit of capital that lies at the heart of the market and of ongoing neocolonial conquest. We need a spirituality that employs other symbols, a spirituality that makes us compose with the land, that teaches us to hear the many voices of the earth, that helps us honor and respond to the spirit/Spirit/s of the land, that compels us to consider the movements of the earth and to tune our senses to the land around us, to the land's own cycles and tempos. The land offers us its own symbols; paying attention to its spirits, to the animation present throughout the earth, leads us to attend to the needs of people, animals, waters, and entire ecosystems. For this kind of spirituality, no idea exists without a body and nobody lacks an idea, it entails compassion and standing in solidarity, movement, and composition with anyone being exploited by the spirituality of the fetish. The compassion that comes from undoing the fetishized separation of thought and embodiment is essential to ending colonial power and the spiritualities it constructs.

Eduardo Viveiros de Castro helps us see how our view of modernity shapes our current spiritual and corporeal worlds.[155] He says that we Westerners understand ourselves and relate to the world from two dimensions. First, the corporeal dimension, which is the dimension of the universal. We are all made of the same materials, carbon atoms, bits of DNA. As embodied creatures, we communicate with all living beings, and we see ourselves as related to chimpanzees, earth creatures, and the elements. Second is the spiritual dimension, which is composed of our soul, mind, and cognitive abilities. According to the contemporary Western understanding, he says, this spiritual dimension is often considered the distinguishing feature of human beings, for only we possess culture and soul. Human materiality is a sort of surplus to that otherworldly, radically transcendent spiritual dimension, an add-on that results from people being made in the image of God.[156]

Our uniqueness as humans thus lies in our spiritual dimension, or head, or soul. While the bodily dimension connects us and encourages us to see our similarities, the spiritual/mental aspect distinguishes not only one individual from another but one culture from another. We even make distinctions within knowledge itself, the human sciences focusing on the spirit and the natural sciences attending to material bodies and phenomena. Viveiros says that this Western tendency to separate and isolate forms of knowing means humans feel no need to plant our feet on the ground; we assume our culture allows us to float somewhere up above it. The result is planetary destruction.

For example, the Christian faith is characterized by its embrace of species exception: God only loves humans. Although animals are an expression of God's love for us, they themselves are not recipients of God's true love. There is no place in heaven for nonhumans, and as we know, the earth will be left behind. Spiritualities shaped by this sort of faith and these sorts of dichotomies must be challenged. In the words of Jewish theologian Abraham J. Heschel, "The divorce of liturgy and living, or prayer and practice, more than a scandal, it is a disaster."[157] We are living with that scandal, and our disasters are right before our eyes: climate catastrophe, economic inequality, and political fascism are just a few. In divorcing our spirituality from the life of the earth, we have abandoned the understanding that, as Thich Nhat Hanh said, "we inter-are with one another and with all life."[158]

We have forgotten that everything we are and do is intimately connected to the ways we engage with the earth. Every ritual prayer, every piece of legislation, every action we take that affects mountains, oceans, and plants, will come back to us one way or another; the spirits of the land will avenge our attacks upon them. Kopenawa explained in a 2023 lecture that "What you call climate change we call the revenge of mother earth."[159] The spirituality of the fetish leads us to believe that the earth is not alive, that there are no spirits of territories and ecologies, rivers, and mountains. But when we engage in wholesale environmental destruction, we feed the spirit of the fetish and turn our backs to the spirit of the land, which then withholds from us what we need.

On both an individual and collective level, spiritual life is critical. Without spirit, politics, ecology, economics, legislation, and education are all reduced to means of control meant to serve only one of earth's species: the human. The question then becomes: what spirit(s) must guide us today? To put it simply, the spirit of the land; the spirit(s) of the earth; the gods of each bioregion; the spirit(s) that orients symbiotic processes of life; the law of the land within each territory; and the lore of the land that combines skies, earth, animals, humans, and more than humans: trees, vegetation, waters, and so on.

But in order to understand the spirit of the land, we must pay attention! And that is how rituals are essential: they direct us to pause and pay attention. We attend to the core of our own bodies, where our spirits live: that is, our breath. That ritual of attendance may take the form of prayer and breathing otherwise known as a poem. As US poet Ada Limón says, "Poems are like trees in this way. They let us breathe together. In each line break, caesura, and stanza, there's a place for us to breathe...poems can be a place to stop and remember that we too are living."[160] Prayer—whether shaped into a poem or not—then becomes a form of hearing and heeding the spirit as we breathe together, connecting our thinking, feeling, and doing; our bodies, territories, words, and world.

And then we start to realize that all people, trees, plants, animals, and oceans breathe. Not only that, we recognize that those plants, our first providers of oxygen, continue to make it possible for us to breathe at all. Along with the oceans, sequestering so much deadly carbon dioxide, they are our caregivers.[161] If the plants stop breathing, if the oceans stop breathing, we die! If we tear down the trees, we die; if animals can no longer play their roles in maintaining the environment, we die. As Covid taught us, we cannot think that the inability of Indigenous and Black and poor communities to breathe will only be contained within those communities; if they die, so too will we. Gaining awareness through our prayers of all these relationships and more, everything begins to change. We breathe not individually, but together; each individual act of living and breathing is in fact *breathing with* every other being on earth. With that revolutionary re-cognition, we also understand that the incarcerated must be free to breathe; that Indigenous communities must be free from government actions that continue to destroy their bodies–territories–worlds. We know that animals must be freed from factory farms and oceans no longer subjected to extractivist fishing practices. We realize that the mountains will only be free to breathe when we cease to mine them; that soils will only choke under the rule of agribusiness and all the chemicals and toxins it uses.

*

But will this recognition really lead to change? Since I have written so much on prayer, people often ask me if I believe in it. I respond that for me, prayer is a ritual, which like any ritual is paradoxical. On the one hand, prayers do nothing. As Heschel says, "We pray in order to pray," and that is pretty much it; nothing else.[162] Prayer is not a utilitarian tool that will save us or anyone else; I pray just because I need to pray, an activity with no necessary meaning, no goal, no desire. It is a necessary action. In fact, prayer is never a transaction. We don't pray to become powerful, to get or to find some object or gift or reward. Coming to prayer with those intentions means engaging in capitalist prayer, a fetishized, merchandised prayer of the market. Engaging in that type of financialized prayer, a fetish that only wears the guise of real prayer, only means spinning in circles.

On the other hand, I do believe wholeheartedly in prayer! It is a powerful ritual! Prayer starts by allowing us to build a house within ourselves, "an established residence," as Heschel says, "for the innermost self. All things have a home, the bird has a nest, the fox has a hole, the bee has a hive [...] the soul, after roaming through a world festered with aimlessness, false-hoods and absurdities, seeks a moment in which to gather up its scattered life."[163] Prayer is our protection in a world of abandonment. And once we have a home where we can take shelter, we are ready to reach out to the often frightening world. In this sense, prayer is able to counter the powers of destruction, overthrow tyrants, turn the world upside down, and bring peace to violent places. Prayer turns despair to hope and finds life where there had only been death. For the disenfranchised, prayer may well be the only weapon available. And when prayer is a collective engagement of one person with other lives, a syncing with the ebb and flow of life, it starts to reveal its true power, which should never be underestimated. When these connections are established, life bursts forth, revealing a web of sustenance made up of a variety of life-forms. Prayer can open up horizons of possibilities never seen before.

To pray, then, is to learn how to live at the heart of a paradox! Prayer is a means of constantly disentangling ourselves from the forms of death that breathe within and around us—so to pray truly, we must detach ourselves from forms of only apparent belonging and embrace genuine forms of relationship. For example, when Potawatomi scientist Robin Wall Kimmerer teaches us to "braid sweetgrass," to establish personal relationships with plants, she is showing us how to reorient our hearts' desires and so is teaching us to truly pray.[164] This call for with-ness with plants is also apparent in the Buddhist concept of witness consciousness—another form of prayer.[165] To return to Heschel, he reminds us that prayer is inextricably connected with our ways of being in the world: "As my prayers, so is my understanding."[166]

Thus, prayers are fundamental to our spiritualities, whatever forms they take. For prayer carries a spirit, moves the spirit, is called by the spirits. Prayer is the soul's invitation to live with the earth as its co-guardian. It builds a home in which all of us can live. Here is how Heschel describes this home: as "more than an exclusive habitat, mine and never yours. A residence devoid of hospitality is a den or a hole, not a home. Prayer must never be a citadel for selfish concerns, but rather a place for deepening concern over other people's plight."[167]

This is how prayer sustains and encourages a spirituality that demands we be warriors. Warriors who will take to the streets and demand transformation. Warriors who won't give up until every incarcerated person is free, every river is clean, every inch of soil is free from pesticides and poison, until fossil fuels remain in the ground. Rising against the powers that keep these changes from happening is an inherent part of our green freedom spirituality.

Ritual embraces both the prayer and the one who prays it. And it is a ritual that will help a spirituality of freedom take the shape and forms of our relationship with the *nomos* of the *oikos* (eco-nomia): the laws of the household, the economy of our living together. Kimmerer reminds us that we can live in accordance with a *gift economy* found in many native traditions, an economy expressly opposed to the market-based, profit-driven economy of settler-colonial capitalism. Whereas a market economy prioritizes and works to serve the sale of commodities and the growth of profits, a gift economy is centered on and serves the relationship between beings, a relationship based on reciprocity that always acknowledges the richness of the land.[168] The land provides for us, and in return, we care deeply for the land. In this way, spirituality is a circular process that moves with the earth, a process in which our bodies, senses, understanding, and intuition become ever more connected with the land, with the elements, with the beings living with us in our shared spaces.

*

I have described, then, two forms of prayers and spiritualities: one of the fetish and one of the earth. Two very different spirits! We could say that one spirituality is attached to the market and another to the land, to the soil, to the waters, to the elements, to the insects, animals, planktons, fungi, to every living being on earth. The spirituality of the market demands money, internal and external development, accomplishment, titles, and rank. It demands more than the earth can give in order that very few people profit. On the other hand, the spirituality, or better said, spiritualities of the earth says that the land must be tended, allowed to go at its own pace; that the water and the seeds that it hosts must be cared for; that the soil must be allowed to breathe and maintain its natural fertility; that we seek permission from the land that allows us to plant and harvest. It respects and moves with the currents of the oceans, in the presence of the moon. This spirituality/ies recognizes insects' roles in sustaining the earth; animals' right to live their full cycles of life; the need to maintain the entire biome in which we live so that we can breathe, eat, work, rest, dream about our land, tell stories, and celebrate.

The spiritualities of the land are obviously very different from the spirituality of the market, which demands private ownership, profit at all cost, monocropping practices, and the maintenance of monocultural societies. The spirituality of the land, on the other hand, reminds us that the earth owns us, that the spirits of the land orient us, that plants are our caretakers, that water is our source of life, that soils are just as fragile as our bodies, that animals are creatures we must honor and protect just as we do humans. In sum, these land-based spiritualities to be found in each bioregion require that we be guardians of the earth; it operates according to an integral, deeply woven, continually mutual movement of culture and nature. US novelist, poet, environmental activist, and farmer Wendell Berry points toward a spirituality of the land when he describes farming:

> Farming involves intelligence, wisdom, devotion, love, compassion, freedom, wildness, harmony, health. It raises urgent questions about economic justice, propriety of scale, harmony between nature and human economy or wildness and cultivation. And all these concerns and considerations, to the limited extent that they can be thought about, can be resolved only in the art of farming a particular farm.[169]

Spirituality, then, does not keep count of the number of prayers one offers; it is not a record of one's adherence to a moral code or proof of one's piety. Rather, spirituality *is* the full life of all beings, the sacredness of the earth—and this in contrast to the false belief in *a* sacred land or sacred people, separated from other lands and peoples. As Wendell Berry says,

> There are no unsacred places;
> there are only sacred places
> and desecrated places.[170]

Thus, to live out these spiritualities is to make sacred again what has been desecrated. For spirituality is the ability to live with the land, hearing the voices of the land, the spirits, and the subjectivities that fill every landscape. If we live in line with this assumption, the spirit/Spirit/s of the earth will lead us not into an allegiance with capitalism but to a connection with the land. The spirit/Spirit/s of the soil, of the wind, of the water, and of the fire, will deliver us from loyalties to nation-states and lead us to devotion to a larger democracy, one that entails all peoples: people–trees, people–insects, people–birds, people–water, people–humans, people–dreams and so on. Spirituality then means movements that correspond with the soul of the land, with the presence of the ancestors in that land, with the thriving of the host of beings that surround us. It means following the desire to be guided by land-oriented patterns and processes, understanding our human roles as guardians of the land, and understanding ourselves as people who have learned and live according to the land's desires. It is also what is at stake in this ritual and these practices, the reorientation of desires, the shifting of love and longing, akin to what Félix Guattari said: "The question is: will a production of desire, a dream, a loving practice, a concrete utopia one day end up achieving, on a social level, the same dignity of existence as a commercial production of cars or canned goods?"[171]

To dream with the land, to desire with the land, to live with the land is to live according to the ancestral knowledge humans have fashioned over the course of millennia. To recreate our past is our way to orient our future. We must fight against the spirit of capitalism that promises a better future severed from the past, having progress as our landmark, carrying a teleological goal where technology will save us all. Against the future as progress, we must understand time not as linear process with an end, but time as spiraling, sinuous widening time that envelops us and circles us as beginning, middle and beginning again. That is what we learn from Antonio Bispo dos Santos, a quilombola thinker from Brazil. He explains this spiraling time: "We are people of journeys, not people of theory. We are of circularity: beginning, middle, and beginning again. Our lives have no end. The grandmother's generation is the beginning, the mother's generation is the middle, and the granddaughter's generation is the beginning again."[172] He explains further elsewhere:

> In Euro-Christian monotheistic society, the grandparent generation has no value. The family is understood as mother-father-child. And this has a biblical basis, because God is a father, but not a grandfather. The cosmology of these people has a beginning, middle, and end. We have a beginning, middle, and beginning again. Euro-Christian society puts the grandfather in a nursing home and the grandchild in daycare. The quilombola people respect the elders and the children.[173]

This spiral entanglement with time demands a deep care for people and the land for the fullness of life to keep happening. Time, land, and people move within the spiraling of life in endless processes of transformation. This relation with time does not wait for progress to arrive but instead, makes the past a site of constant remaking. Thus, in this ongoing movement between grandparents and children, we remake the kinship with the land, with other species and with the notion of peoples who were not and are not captured by the spirit of capitalism or any notion of nation-states. Spiraling with the land, we instantiate ourselves in new impossibilities for a new world to arrive. Brazilian scholar Leda Maria Martins speaks of this spiraling time in her book *Performances of Spiral Time*:

> As a call and response, time ebbs and flows in spirals, reinaugurating us in its kinesis. In the turns of time, we are. Ntangu time for the Bantu-Kongo people, sunlight time, time crossed in the wind, embodied experienced time. Time that echoes into other times, whether in the act of dissemination or the act of retreat.[174]

Shifting our thinking/feeling/relating with the land, we might open spaces for other desires to flourish, other feelings to circulate, another unconscious to appear, and other symptoms to manifest. If we reforest our imagination, then we might start dreaming with the rivers, with the forest, with the land, with animals, with our ancestors, and not only with our locked selves, dreaming of a new car or a new thing to buy. If the land becomes the ground and horizon of our living, our boredom will be received by the land and not by online stores and shopping malls. The future will not consist of the effort to get the latest new toys but rather, to live in accordance with the older ways that once showed us how to exist fully. By engaging the future as spiral, our past as ancestralities can challenge our assumption that the good life means infinite economic growth, and we can finally realize that living according to the limits of the earth will ensure that all beings can enjoy the possibility of full life.

Thus, my spirit and my spiritual life are bound to the spiraling flux and movements of the earth, spirit/Spirit/s of the land and the material life of the bodies, territories, and worlds within each bioregion. My prayer in this time will be done toward the East but also toward the West, toward the South and toward the North, composing all times together. My spiritual life is indeed bound to the earth's vitality and its movements. Kimmerer says that "we make a grave error if we try to separate individual well-being from the health of the whole."[175] When one suffers, everyone suffers; when one is alive, everyone is alive. That is the heart of any earthly spirituality.

CHAPTER NINETEEN

Molecular Revolutions

Now we turn to French philosopher Félix Guattari's concept of "molecular revolution"—small-scale transformations that work at the micro-level of daily life, desire, and subjectivity. This concept helps us understand how our three simple gestures can create the kind of change we desperately need. Molecular revolutions happen in the everyday: in how we perceive, in how we relate, in the small practices that reshape our environment and our subjectivities. From there, we can hope for large-scale revolutions. Let me explain how this works and why it matters for our ritual practice.

In this age of all possible crises, political fascism, and financial and fossil-fuel capitalism, the natural world faces annihilation, the climate is in chaos, and the very balance of the planet is at risk. Our lives are headed straight for the abyss of destruction. But we can and must change this situation.

When we think about climate disasters, we tend to believe they inherently come along because humans, all of us, have caused it. It feels as if there is no other possible form of life because there is no way to move away from capitalism and its only form of living. But none of this is true. Our crisis comes from the exploitation of the earth by 1 percent of the population. It comes from big corporations that control most of the resources of the planet. However, we can and must respond to the crises we face right where we live, trying to create alternative ways of living together, social arrangements not centered around money, profit, and domination, but upon the earth. We can create these new social arrangements by engaging in molecular revolutions where we are, fostering new ways of living to come to life; by expanding and connecting with other molecular movements around us, thus creating the possibility of many new worlds living together. And that is only possible when we connect with the bioregion where we live, developing a spirituality of relationship.

That spirituality, encouraging and encouraged, sustaining and sustained by the ritual of rising, bowing, and prostrating, can both break through the walls of capitalism by re-ligare, that is, reconnecting "individual" selves to larger collections of life, such as present and future bioregions. But for that to happen, for us to be able to understand rituals as full political movements of transformation and creation of new forms of existence, we must come to a clear awareness of the forces that have shaped us and that we are up against: coloniality, land theft, plantation-based enslavement, and transformation into property and sources of profit of people, animals, and earth. These are the same forces that persist within current practices of financial capitalism, corporations, banks, and multinational mining and fossil fuel corporations, not to mention agribusiness's exploitative, white-supremacist monocropping, and animal monoculturing.

This capitalistic form of existence has been supported and maintained by vast structures of power and domination through hierarchy, patriarchy, racism for too long: competition and exploitation of relations between humans, animals, and everything on earth; desires related to personal gain and owning private property; class divisions; monetary and fiscal policies disconnected with the pace of the land; strangling of communities' agency; development and profit-based economic politics; cultural institutions organized without the natural world; educational systems uprooted from the earth; religious beliefs, rituals, and worship detached from the time-space of the land, and so on.

It has been very difficult for any form of large-scale revolution to occur. But small revolutions are always possible, living as we seem to be in the time of Guattari's micropolitics and molecular revolutions, described earlier.[176] For Guattari, these revolutions, intended to shatter capitalism and create new living arrangements, are steeped in Marxism and a form of inquiry known as schizoanalysis. That is, his aim is to connect philosophy and political action in order to derail the patterns and processes of capitalism. For him, molecular revolution engages both the objective outward work of transformation while also and more fundamentally demanding the production of subjectivities able to respond to capitalism's own tailor-made subjectivities. Guattari attests that capitalist forces "understand that the production of subjectivity is possibly more important than any other kind of production, more essential than the production of petroleum and energy."[177] Thus, for molecular revolution to happen, it must be able to produce subjectivity through both conscious and unconscious desire. Desire, then, is key to the creation of subjectivity—and importantly, is collectively shaped as "all forms of the will to live, the will to create, the will to love, the will to invent another society, another perception of the world, and other value systems."[178]

These two notions, subjectivity and desire, are fundamental to understanding rituals' power and force. Rituals are a privileged place for producing different forms of subjectivity since they work on both conscious and unconscious levels; hence, they can serve as portals for all sorts of will and desire. Moreover, as ritual leads us to many forms of relationship with humans and all other beings in our bioregions, the spiritual connections that are created make possible the emergence of a plethora of subjectivities and desires. Since molecular revolutions are embodied social processes that create life, rituals-as-molecular revolutions are social processes in which the bodies of many species are entangled, creating the possibilities of many, always interrelated forms of life.

Moreover, for Guattari, for an anticapitalist revolution to occur it must be molecular, moving in various directions at the same time, connecting people, ideas, and, I would add, *spirit/Spirit/s* acting at the level of deep local relationship that will transform capitalism at its very root. Guattari says it clearly in an interview:

> There is always a small margin, a small possibility. At your university, you have some colleagues, some friends. You have the possibility of creating an enunciative group that will perhaps find echoes and correspondences. And so, these very local, very micropolitical dimensions may be in harmony with phenomena of molecular mutation on another scale. Because today, after all, it is the most local that communicates the most planetary. It is worrying about the defense of the trees that Chirac wants to cut down in Paris, taking care of the defense of animals, the defense of the biosphere, fighting against pollution, all of this immediately resonates with "What is this way of being on the planet?" Do men believe that their existence in the universe is as if they were under the eyes of God, or as a gift from God, as a creation of God? And this excludes all responsibility towards the biosphere, towards the cosmos, towards being. And now, we say that today through these small microscopic acts, "you are responsible for what is happening," you have ethical-political responsibilities in relation to the future. Not only the future of human life, but of the planet, the future of all animal species, the future of the biosphere, the future of species, I would even say the future of being itself.[179]

It is this very notion of molecular revolution that we are claiming in this book. Through intentional rituals and gestures created and practiced everywhere, done in known and unexpected places, relationships will be formed within the landscapes we inhabit, establishing forms of connection that will bring us to consciousness of ourselves with others, as others, and to a desire to take care of each other and protect each other's worlds. Other practices, desires, connections, and relationships can also help create other unconscious forms of imagining and fabulating the world.

If capitalism is the practice of cruelty, these gestures are practices of care. Capitalism is about capturing subjectivities in order to desire desire itself, whereas these rituals can create subjectivities that desire to care for others. Capitalism creates pedagogies of cruelty, teaching us to hate, to abandon places and people, to live in precarity, to adapt ourselves to brutality and scarcity.[180] But we, on the other hand, can create pedagogies of care that teach us to connect, to relate, to protect, and to empathize, producing what is enough for all, respecting the limits of the land. Pedagogies of healing that reject the destruction of people and all living beings.

Since they must be done in the places we find ourselves, these rituals provide us a deeper sense of belonging and then of agency as well, sparking many forms of molecular revolution that, entangled with other people and living beings, can transform entire systems and modes of existence.

These ritual gestures carry an intentionality that will help create, imagine, invent, engender, fabulate, and enact many forms of relationship and change. As we engage in the ritual, we both enact and are enacted by it: whatever we do will return to do something in and to us. For example, when I started to pay attention to the ways wild animals live near my house, I also started to pay attention to the ways they die. But then unexpectedly, I started to notice instances of roadkill, recognizing the massive number of animals killed on our streets, roads, and highways. I started researching and looking for people invested in caring for animals hit and killed by cars. When I began reading about how animals die and how they mourn each other, I began moving their bodies from the road and giving them proper burials, singing and saying a prayer. I even carry bags and gloves now in my car for this purpose. Never did I imagine that practicing the three-gesture ritual I've described would lead me to this place.

Even though we are intentional about carrying out our rituals, they affect us in unexpected, unconsidered ways. That constant movement allows rituals to act as molecular revolutions that will orient and reorient our attention to a plethora of necessary political actions. Rituals are then outwardly directed molecular revolutions that also work on a molecular level within us, changing us deeply. As Guattari says, this circular flow of affections can restore our relationship with the earth and bring us to a deeper consciousness of and responsibility for planetary life. With these gestures, even initially, we are able to break the hold of detached lifestyles and begin the journey back to what we are made of and give us life: water, soil, air, fire, and spirit/Spirit/s.

What is fundamental to Guattari's understanding of molecular revolution is its focus on the correlation between social and subjective transformation. As we remind ourselves of our relationship with other subjects—plants, birds, waters, rocks, and more—we might be able to explode our sense of the discrete self, the assumption that my self only exists within this separate being that I am, independent from the rest of the world. We could then see ourselves as multiple, as parts of a larger landscape: the birds that sing are myself, the rivers that run near my home are myself, the soil where my food is grown is myself. Those correlations and correspondences force us to understand that we cannot continue to live as we have been living: polluting the air that will destroy the birds and the rivers and the soils that are myself. The workings of our exploitative and profit-driven industries and economies, our understanding of work itself: all of it must change. Social transformation occurs when we reject the demand that we continue to live in line with the assumptions of profit and economic development.

Thus, and in contrast to Guattari, my aim is not to achieve a fully *autonomous* self, but a self that is deeply dependent—and not dependent on machines, bosses, or the economy as we know it, but rather, dependent in the sense of relating deeply to human and more than human beings, to the earth as a whole but especially where we live, for a life well lived. Or as the Quechua People say: *Sumak kawsay*. A life lived well is a life oriented by the land. The understanding of the law, of the nomos, shifts from being my own self-law, my own self-determination, to something much larger, that is, to belonging to countless networks that make up the law of the land. For I *am* the entire landscape I am a part of, not a discrete, autonomous self.[181]

I want to hold on to Guattari's assertion in *The Lines Of Flight*: "A new type of struggle is trying to find its feet, less as a model than as a demonstrable 'precedent' that another field of possibility is well and truly open."[182] Rituals *are* this way of finding our feet, our bodies, of moving into the full depth of our present crises in order to discover there a field of possibilities, a way in and through them. Rituals provide a way of living among monsters, between, as Italian philosopher Antonio Gramsci would say, the ghosts that have left us and the ones who have not arrived.[183] In this time in which we live, our circumstances demand not only understanding but change, a combination of feeling-thinking-doing to respond to and transform we-two, the planet and myself, the planet as me.

In finding our feet, we access different modes of relation, including those we fundamentally cannot control. One source of our current peril stems from the acceptance of modernity's assumption that we can only live well if we feel we are in control—of people, time, events, the past, the future, work, feelings... German sociologist Hartmut Rosa points to "modernity's incessant desire to make the world engineerable, predictable, available, accessible, disposable (i.e., verfügbar) in all its aspects. And...this very desire alters our relationship to the world."[184]

Almost every aspect of our lives, including our desires, is fabricated. Showbusiness, sports, and religion: all aim at some form of control. Even education has been boiled down to a mere enterprise of goals, objectives, and learning outcomes. And our desire for control paradoxically increases the risk that everything will be destroyed. As Rosa says,

> this desire for control produces, behind our backs, a world that in the end is utterly uncontrollable in all the relevant aspects. We cannot control our late modern world in any way: politically, economically, legally, technologically, or individually. The drive and desire toward controllability ultimately creates monstrous, frightening forms of uncontrollability.[185]

In other words, the path to destruction is marked by our fear of being unable to control everything around us: our bodies, our partners, our families, our religions, our politics, our food, our thoughts,... This desperation leads us to create and adopt innovations and technologies, political ideologies, ritual actions, and inward-focused forms of relationship that are harmful to ourselves and the earth.

To counter these forms of living, thinking, moving, and desiring, we must think about forms of revolution. Again, not big revolutions but rather small ones, micropolitical ones. In that way, rituals can be one other source of revolution. Paul B. Preciado helps us think about the concept of revolution:

> The revolution hypothesis brings together a series of ideas, citations and practices coming from anti-colonial movements aiming to take steps towards a new earthly epistemology. The word revolution is not an ideological slogan or a partisan diktat, but a utopian organization of political desire, an exercise in cognitive emancipation, a speculative fabulation, in Donna Haraway's words: a counter narrative that seeks to modify the perspective on what is happening, to change the questions in order to propose new answers. To imagine is already to act: to recover the imagination as a force for political transformation is already to begin to mutate.[186]

So we begin by counteracting present assumptions with ritual practices able to shift our cognition, our perceptions, our perspective, our desires; able to open up planes of immanence and allow us experience the fullness of presence right in front of us, in the tracks of opossums or the stars that shine in our part of the sky.[187] These fields of immanence are presences meeting other presences, other life-forms, creating encounters that do and undo each other, shifting, producing, transforming, reproducing, and dissipating each other.

Sharing my own experience may help illustrate how this happens. When I began paying attention to the earth, engaging in the gestures of rising, bowing, and prostrating, I had no idea how much that attention would change me. Now I can't start my day without first listening to the birds. And driving now is painful, because as I said before, every time I see a dead animal by the side of the road, I stop whenever possible to move it away from the paved area to allow other animals to eat or to mourn. Attending to the earth has shifted my desires, my cognition, my perspective, my perceptions and forms of relation, my practices, my sense of withness. The three-part ritual's inherent receptivity to change and unstructured repetition means it bears within it a resistance to being controlled. As such, it may provide a way, as it has for me, of opening ourselves up to new forms of being, of being-with. This withness might shift our consciousness, allowing other desires to come forth and change the way we move through the world. But this withness is loaded with power dynamics of which we must be aware. Theologian Joerg Rieger calls our attention to the importance of agency and power:

> At stake is more than a methodological issue. Scholars of religion and theology will not be able to recognize alternative forms of religion unless they take into account the history of how power is shaped and reshaped in particular material social relations and social movements. As a result, we need to pay closer attention to whose agency matters in what ways and who benefits and who does not in a given system—keeping in mind the agency of both people and nature.[188]

And we do need to change the ways we think about and enact the movements of power and agency. We need different forms of agency and different social actors to look up to: not the gold digger or the merchant, the salesman or the lauded economist who contributes to infinite market growth. Instead, we need urban ecological watchers, water and animal protectors, forest warriors, fossil-fuel fighters, caregivers for rivers, mountain guardians, plant lovers, stewards of bioregions: different types of earth guardians. Moreover, we need to see that every living being carries some form of agency and is a guardian of their own environment. Thus, it is the composition of many guardians that can keep the well-being of a bioregion.

Alongside these guardians, we also need, as Brazilian poet and theologian Rubem Alves suggests, poets, warriors, and prophets.[189] In line with Ada Limón's claims above, poets able to perceive and share the wonder in everything. Warriors to fight corporations that are killing us and prophets to continue insisting that this way of living is wrong and that our current approach to existence will not hold much longer. Theological and religious reasoning alone won't be enough; lectures and books won't suffice. And neither will mere feeling nor an isolated spiritual routine. If we lean too far toward a single practice or tendency, blinding ourselves to the fullness of the collective world, we run the risk of becoming dry, self-righteous people; poets who can only see themselves in the mirrors of their poems; weak and inconsequential warriors; prophets of their own mirrors.

New Yorker Bill Talen, aka Reverend Billy, is a mix of poet, warrior, and prophet. Revivalist preacher and pastor of the Church of Stop Shopping, his work is dedicated to anticonsumerist communion. In addition to providing accompaniment at regular Sunday worship services, the church's choir also performs rituals on the streets and in churches, casting out demons from Starbucks and backing Reverend Billy's fervent preaching.[190] These performances, done in different places with different public and specific issues, are ritualizing forms that bring awareness intended to lead to change and transformation. These performances may create different forms of awareness than the ones proposed in this book. But they speak to the same attempt to break the chains of the capital. Their intention is not to move us out into our various terrains—but they provide critical lenses for viewing our normalized habits and our attachments to consumerism and brands, our attachment to, for example, the obscene prices of Starbucks's coffee. And I am not concerned with these performances' achievement of "proper" results, for art cannot be measured according to the expectations of people or numbers.

But no ritual gesture becomes a revolution if there is only the work of an individual. Individual gestures must become larger movements of collective action and transformation. Only groups, even if small, can keep the flame of change alive. Philosopher Jean Tible helps us think about this relationship by talking about wild politics.[191] Tible thinks about politics not only in what we recognize as official places for politics, also rather, in every gesture, movement, and life lived everywhere. Politics is on the streets, in the demonstrations of the people who fight for justice and emancipation everywhere. Politics is in the brutality of the police against a movement of emancipation, in the square where we gather, in the places where we work, in the places where inequality and poverty massacre human and every other form of life, and in the forest where our deepest sustenance comes from, in the small rural areas where family farmers are trying to survive, and in the large monoculture concerns dominated by agribusiness. Tible, then, traces movements of rebellion and revolt everywhere! In other words, he sees molecular revolutions happening in every corner of history, whether official or subjugated: in Black liberation movements, LGBTQIA+ demonstrations, the campaigns of the Brazilian street cleaners known as Margaridas, and the work of Indigenous Peoples who carry, in his words, a "spirit-practice" that guides the defense of the forest and thus, of every place where life, human and more than human, is present.[192] For Tible, the land is also a political agent that fosters wild politics. If so, we could say that floods, droughts, tsunamis, catastrophes, the alteration of atmospheric cycles, and more, are all forms of rebellion, bioregional revolt against the abuse and exploitation of the earth. We must listen, then, to what these rebellions are telling us, and change our habits and assumptions accordingly.

The gestures in this book want to be a part of the wild politics Tible describes. If we become deeply involved with the land, we will have no other choice but to fight for its life. This ritual will then *place us* in a space where we can offer models of rebellion against all forms of destruction of our extensive, multiple, and rich bioregions, creating molecular revolutions of many forms, shapes, and orientations. These wild political irruptions and disruptions will lead us to new ways of thinking about our common worlds and the ways we inhabit them.

Rituals blur the realms of public and private into which the world has been artificially split. This reenvisioning makes every space a common one, a nature-culture space, allowing us to learn how to become the living landscape. In this way, rituals find ways of continuously disrupting the strictures of colonial nation-state politics. Rituals, as understood here, see boundaries not as political lines that indicate geographical possession but as markers between differently configured bioregions. They erase the need for hierarchical powers of domination, revealing to us instead the power of horizontal gatherings that do not designate one species as being more important than another but they work in a confluence of mutual service. They work to repair brokenness by reviving alternative epistemologies and forms of knowing that were almost destroyed. Rituals allow us to understand that living in community is living in relationship, where life is understood as multiple forms being integrated into patches of whole, and where no one overwhelms or excludes the presence of the others.

Over time, weaving together rituals and recovered knowledges, practicing gestures such as rising–bowing–prostrating, can lead to different forms of relationships able to foster a new sort of democracy. One in which the *demos*—the people—are valued, and in which the very concept of demos is expanded. To engage in ritual is to gather, so to speak, the demos-humans, demos-trees, demos-plants, demos-insects, demos-waters, and so on. That is what a real democracy should mean! Humans could then create bioregion embassies, with councils representing every species: something akin to Bruno Latour's "parliament of things," which is a form of relationship in which nonhumans have a voice in democratic life.[193] However, as many criticisms of this concept have shown, we must still search for ways of reconfiguring and reorienting power, economies, epistemologies, and politics. Indigenous thinker and author Ailton Krenak, from the Krenak people, summarizes the challenge:

> The individualized subject results by separating the human from their relationship with place as a support for life. Political ecology, through the counter-hegemonic epistemology we propose, is a project that reconstructs this relationship between collective subjects and the organic existence they hold in common; it exposes the asymmetrical structures of power that affect this common subject/environment relationship and promote individualization/dispossession. . . . Individualism separated from an ecological relationship with place leads to the promotion of enclosure, privatization and appropriation of collective projects of existence on a common planet. . . .The idea of nature separated from collective subjects is the result of this abysmal colonial violence manifesting as an ecological imbalance.[194]

We may think of Isabelle Stengers's proposal of a new cosmopolitics, which focuses on human interconnectedness and a variety of perspectives, experiences, and shared knowledges brought together in a spirit of "speculative engagement" to transform political processes and challenge power asymmetries.[195] Even so, we need not have these theories and proposals at the front of our minds when we begin to perform the three-part ritual I lay out here. It is enough to start by simply rising, bowing, and prostrating ourselves surrounded by the singular beings of one's bioregion.

In time, the ritual may bring us to the realization that justice, freedom, and love cannot exist, much less flourish, if only a small group of people own the land. As we pay attention to the strictures and structures that restrict land ownership to a comparative few, we might understand the need to fight for the ability for everyone to freely inhabit, work upon, care for, and be responsible for a parcel of land, to act as good guardians of that bit of earth. The practice of ritual, then, can indeed nurture and engender a molecular revolution, can lead us to what Paulo Freire would call the dialogic pedagogy of action and reflection.[196] We start with a ritual, and as we grow in our awareness of the surrounding terrain, with all the injustices and wonders it contains, we move together to bring down capitalism, to break down nation-states, to dismantle ownership of private properties, and to demand agrarian reform.

Of course, this hope is unambiguously naïve, devastatingly so—and yet we must hold on to this stretched horizon, this naïveté, faith or stubbornness, as molecular revolutions start to pop up everywhere. As we continue to repeat these ritual gestures, these molecular revolutions will in turn enact big changes not only of individual perspective and understanding but of collective forms of existence. We may come to see, for example, that it is the law of the land, not human jurisprudence or the state, that should determine the course of life. With that realization, we must then work out how jurisprudence can operate according to that law. As we continue down this path, the boundaries that mark our environments will no longer be those artificially imposed by the state, but by the natural confines of different bioregions. The communities that inhabit a particular place will not only be understood as including the diversity of people who live there, but also all species found there, gathered together into a common society where land belongs not just to landowners, but to all, human and more than human. Until we realize that it is the land that owns us, that the earth has always owned us, and that we are only guardians of the land, tending, attending to, caring for, and honoring the gifts of the earth.

But for that to happen, we must repeat the gestures of this ritual one hundred thousand times over, until something in us clicks, and we start to change, and be changed, move and be moved, shift and be shifted, transform and be transformed. To repeat is to find the ritual, and the places around us, renewed a million times over. That is the challenge. The spirit of capitalism takes away our desire to continue anything. We always need something new to get us out of our boredom. We battle against the spirit of capitalism. The spirit that makes us live only in the evanescence of the present, exhausting ourselves into expectations of intense pleasures and at the same time survival. This spirit takes away our strength, our sustenance, and we end up giving up.

Hopefully, these ritual gestures will start to cleanse us from that spirit of sickness and death and bring us the animated spirit/Spirit/s of the land. With time, we will come to see that our lives and the lives of our communities can indeed engage in economies of mutual care and reciprocity. Once we start, the discernment of the spirit/Spirit/s will be key to understand the balance between the forces of death and the forces of life.

With the spirit/Spirit/s of the land, power will not be wielded in top-down fashion by one person or just a few, but should be shared among all species. Obligation will not be understood as a patriotic duty, but rather as the need to participate in, care for, and be responsible to and for this community of people, animals, plants, waters, and all species within it. Allegiance will not be offered to any flag, but given to the spirit/Spirit/s of the land who guide us. All of these changes will lead to a redistribution of knowledge, power, authority, and, of course, land.

If ritual and its regular practice encompass the concerns of every aspect of our lives—landscapes, stories, love, means of production, lifestyles, caring, and so much more—it can help to foster what Eduardo Viveiros de Castro called "an agrarian reform of Western knowledge" and of the land.[197] Rituals must then be topological movements, ways of lingering in the place we live in order to hear what it has to tell us. The longer we inhabit a space and make it an oikos, a home, the more loudly and clearly that space will speak to us.

As we have seen, rituals can not only disrupt the ways we currently live; they can also help us begin to invent a new form of life. These ritual gestures offer spaces to try out and practice that new life: every time we bow, rise, prostrate ourselves, and go forward into the tasks of our day, we both rehearse and actualize this future. Becoming anew alongside and with the land, we open space in the present for the unthought to arise. This is why I want to caution us *against* understanding ritual as something simply ecologically or politically centered. I am trying instead to get as close as possible to Indigenous ways of being and thinking and doing that emerge through ceremony.[198] These ceremonies are not viewed as discrete ecorituals, political rituals, or religious rituals. This sort of compartmentalization doesn't exist here, where thinking-feeling-doing is living as an inherent part of bodies–territories–worlds. No aspect of reality is excluded from the ceremony; all of life is found within it. For each season, though, there is a ceremony; each need summons a particular ceremony. For non-Indigenous people, then, rituals are ways of moving into thinking-feeling-doing the fullness of life—which means the fullness of all beings: bodies–territories–worlds. Rituals are indeed propellers of molecular revolutions!

FIGURE 6 *How dare you?*

CHAPTER TWENTY

Reorienting Our Common Living

Since we have repeated many times how the individual is always a companion of many beings, and we are always living with others, we can say that the ritual gestures offered here are not just for the benefit of the community or the earth as a whole; they are also aimed at healing one's heart, mind, body, and soul. As each of us practices these ritual gestures, we move inward to learn about ourselves and our own disconnection from the land and our world. It is important to say that these ritual gestures are not intended as "self-help" or something to do to feel good and allow us to go about our lives unscathed. Instead, this ritual moves in cyclical fashion, inward and outward; it is a sacramental circularity that reveals grace, love, and the landscape's fullness of life as it exists in us. That circular movement prompts us to examine where change is needed, the internal and external places where something is not working. It also directs us to protect and guard that which is fully alive in and around us. With their inward and outward focus, these ritual gestures foster peace in relationships by connecting us with the environment around us, motivating us to assume responsibility for the places and people who live alongside us and to fight against all forms of injustice. The aim of these ritual gestures, then, is to transform us into healers, peacemakers, and revolutionaries, beings living with endless presences of other beings.

We might get a better sense of how this happens when we look more closely at what thought is. An individual thought is never an isolated idea or occurrence; it is instead the composite result of collective thinking, nature manifesting itself in us, through us, and beyond us. Ritual is meant to recognize this interwoven thinking, this collective molecular action, and channel it into the practice of micropolitics.

Deleuze and Guattari describe "becoming-minoritarian": a process in which every form of becoming, of changing, of awareness, of close proximity to the earth, can give rise to a revolutionary act, shifting the political imaginary, reorganizing power and enabling that which has been repressed to see the light of day, further altering and recreating forms of relationship. Local action—molecular revolutions—both individual and collective, corresponds with other local actions that then join together in the effort to uphold and care for all life-forms, pressuring local and even national governments, corporations both small and multinational.

Combined with these local actions, ritual gestures that heighten our awareness work to undo the "metabolic rift" discussed by Karl Marx: the alienation of humans from the natural world, an estrangement established by the fetishized, invasive species known as capitalism.[199] In working to heal that rift, these gestures function in line with the notion of religion as religare, rebinding our relationship with the land and with sustainable modes of production and reproduction. This rebinding is indeed a historical change, a new phase of the class struggle that moves, as we shatter systems based on surplus value and profit, as we reject competition in favor of reciprocity, from applying only to humans to all species.

This beyond-human expansion of the struggle is essential. A recent article shows how disproportionately human—as opposed to other species'—activities make demands upon the resources earth is able to provide. Here we see that almost 60 percent of the planet's biomass is made up of animals domesticated to serve human needs. Cattle alone represent 40 percent of all land and marine mammals combined. The dogs we consider pets account for as much as *all* wild terrestrial mammals such as elephants; domesticated pigs constitute the equivalent of all wild marine mammals such as whales. Of Earth's total mammalian biomass, 36 percent is represented by humans.[200]

In these circumstances, we see how human assumptions about both land and ownership have turned the earth into a space meant to serve the interests of a small portion of the planet's inhabitants. But if we continue to live according to these assumptions and the habits they encourage, there will be no future for any of us—humans, other creatures, or the planet itself. Unless we find ways of respecting each other's habitats and of enhancing other species' territories, our current colonizing, capitalist, exploitative, extractivist, and individualistic manner of existence will kill us all.

In contrast to the neoliberal idea of freedom—individual, isolated freedom for the few who can afford ownership of resources both material and legal—real freedom is, and is only possible, if it is freedom for all. I can't be free if someone else is not, if people are imprisoned or animals are caged, if rivers are drained or channeled for hydropower while ignoring the consequences of such actions. Only when we learn how to be free together will freedom ring.

It's not only a question of physical survival; if the beings around me are unwell, unhappy, *I* can't be happy. If it is the case that no justice anywhere is injustice everywhere, or freedom is only possible where everyone is free, the same is true for happiness. I can only be happy if the birds and the owls around me are happy, if the rivers are flowing freely, if donkeys can frolic together in their herds, if bees can play, if animals are safe and comfortable in their own habitats, if the oceans can breathe, if the mountains are joyful, if the chipmunks and the squirrels and the foxes and the coyotes and the jaguars are happy. And none of us can be happy if we live according to the dictates of capitalism, which tell us we must never stop growing, must always strive for domination, and must always act only according to our own exclusive desires. Given the results of research such as the biomass figures above, it is evident that happiness depends, in fact, on *de-growth*, un-progress, and de-development.[201]

Russell Means of the Oglala Lakota Nation lays out the differences between Indigenous, anti-development modes of being and what he calls European logic:

> Being is a sacred proposition. Gaining is a material act. Traditionally, American Indians have always attempted to be the best people they could. Part of that sacred process was and is to give away wealth, to discard wealth in order not to gain. Material gain is an indicator of false status among traditional people, while it is "proof that the system works" to Europeans. Clearly, there are two completely opposing views at issue here... Terms like progress and development are used as cover words here, the way victory and freedom are used to justify butchery in the dehumanization process. For example, a real-estate speculator may refer to "developing" a parcel of ground by opening a gravel quarry; development here means total, permanent destruction, with the earth itself removed. But European logic has gained a few tons of gravel with which more land can be "developed" through the construction of road beds. Ultimately, the whole universe is open—in the European view—to this sort of insanity.[202]

We can confront this sort of insanity and initiate unprocesses by paying attention. Looking at a space filled only with trees and vegetation, I cannot see it as uncultivated wilderness in need of development. Paying attention, I think instead of how wonderful it is that this habitat for so many other beings is still intact. I know that those other creatures deserve a home just as much as I do. Perceiving the world in this way may have the power to infuse our hearts with gratitude, with peace—to awaken us to awe in the most insignificant moments: how wonderful it is that the earth has given me this fruit to eat, this water to drink, this shirt to warm me! With this new sensibility, we begin to see ourselves not as *homo oeconomicus*, but as part of the multispecies, multiform life that inhabits a very diverse earth. Molecular revolution! Means provides some advice as we learn to pay attention in this way:

> Our Ancestors are our constant witness and companion. They know everything. They are part of us, as we are part of them. In this way,

> an American Indian is never a solitary or lonely individual. Existential angst is unknown. We know who we are and we are never alone. We are part of something greater than ourselves... An American Indian is aware that if disgrace or dishonor is brought upon oneself, then our Grandmother Earth has been insulted as well.... It is still not too late. The living Earth can be saved—and with her, the lives of all of us who depend on her. But the Little Brothers will have to change their way of living on the Earth. Otherwise, say the Kogi, their holy mountain will die, and the Little Brothers will bring upon us all the end of all life on Earth.[203]

We can't assume that simply mimicking Indigenous ways—whatever that might mean—will save us. We are not looking to bring back an idealized past or romanticize any particular culture; instead, we witness a people's living according to a certain knowledge of the land, an ancestral wisdom that most of us have lost and that can actually give us all a way forward. Indigenous lifeways provide examples of how to pay attention, and what to attend to. At the same time, Indigenous life in the present is inextricably connected to what has come before—and looking back to that past can prepare us for the future. In the words of Ailton Krenak, our future is ancestral. He describes intergenerational relationships among the Krenak in Brazil:

> Krenak children long to be ancient. This is because among human communities in which children still have the freedom and autonomy to long for worlds, they really value their elders. The elders gain perspective from various stages of life experience. They are the storytellers, those who teach the study of medicine, art, the foundations of everything relevant to having a good life... coveted site of knowledge... Indigenous children are not educated, but guided. They don't learn to be winners, because for some to win, others need to lose. They learn to share the place where they live and what they have to eat. They learn from the model of a life in which the individual counts less than the collective. This is the Indigenous wisdom, a legacy that passes from generation to generation. What our children learn from early on is to put their hearts in the rhythm of the Earth.[204]

To "place our hearts in the rhythm of the earth" is the beginning of all wisdom, a full acknowledgment that the earth has its own ways of being, that those ways provide us a wise pattern for full living. As Vitor Westhelle reminds us, "Land has the greatest moral and spiritual significance, and constitutes a focus for the way of life."[205] To understand and live according to that significance, we must recognize that we cannot take for ourselves the places or beings that belong to the land and the water; we cannot destroy the habitats of millions of other beings. And to understand all of that, we need to discern and accept our own limits.

Among other things, this means learning to think with our senses. Imagine what would happen if we gave full attention to the sounds of the wind, the birds, the insects, the trees. And consider what it would mean to think with our feet; what would it change about where and how we stand, whom we walk with, how we move along our paths? Suely Rolnik tells us that when we walk, we create relationships between the *topoi* on which we stand. Step by step, we then realize that our path is "multiplied and differentiated," constantly being composed and recomposed as we go. Each step is a sort of micropolitical action that recognizes how our desires and/as actions inscribe new creations within the territories we walk; how we continually cross multiple cartographies that can themselves be changed.[206] Fundamentally, that also means engaging in cross-species communication that demands we speak and listen in different languages—human and other than human. It assumes, too, that human discourse-and-listening is only one, and not the main, component of these new relational configurations. Practicing the ritual I describe in this book provides a way to begin learning other species' languages. But for that, I have to walk slowly, paying attention to whether I am stepping on any other being in front of me.

How we walk determines how we live with the land we stand upon, as well as whom we listen to. Look at some of the ways Italian philosopher Giorgio Agamben describes people walking: "The 'man who walks at ordinary speed', the 'man who runs carrying a rifle', the 'woman who walks and picks up a jug', the 'woman who walks and sends a kiss' are the happy and visible twins of the unknown and suffering creatures who left these traces."[207] Each manner of walking adds to and influences different languages, meanings, paces, material things, values, and ultimately forms of relation. Modernity has taught us to run, run without end, all the while babbling in the English we have been taught to accept as the world's lingua franca—but if we are constantly running, we cannot pay attention and we cannot hear anyone speaking. Thich Nhat Hanh described this situation, our present spiritual condition, in a brief anecdote: "A man is riding a horse very fast, running somewhere. A person next to the road screams at him: Where are you going so fast? And the man replies: 'I don't know, ask the horse.'"[208] Most of our running is for nothing, or is the result of fear or simple lack of knowledge about what we're running for or for whom. We must listen to the horse and figure out why *he* is running—and then find a way to run alongside him.

Everyday people, people like us can start making these changes. If we start recycling at home, it's not because that habit will change the world—we know it won't—but because that habit becomes part of our body's stored knowledge. If we take a walk along a nearby river, and think about the river, and become interested in the river, we might trigger a process that includes the river as a fundamental part of our own stories. And as our interest grows, we want to learn more, coming in the process to admire and ultimately love the river. And through this connection, we come back at some point to ourselves. One of my students described this "return" from the land in a paper:

> I found myself repeating the gesture over and over, adding new lines that were my own, as the sun inched over the horizon and the sky turned pink-orange. Every cell in my body came alive, reminding me of the first time that I did the ritual in my backyard. I knew that I was likely responding to the novelty of the moment—the breathtaking beauty of the place. But I also had a strange feeling of being welcomed by the surrounding trees and the birds and the little bunny hopping across the grass nearby. Strangely, I did not feel alone. I felt called outside, beckoned, and welcomed. It felt, for a moment, that I had found community. The natural world around me seemed to desire my presence and every living thing received my ritual gladly.... Ever since I arrived at (this place), I've been gleefully greeting the sunrise with my daily ritual, even when the fog has been so thick that I can't see the sun. And each day, I've gently pressed myself against my favorite tree. Today, when I embraced it, I was reminded that, to borrow Leonardo Boff's words, I am a "member of a larger planetary and cosmic community." (*Cry of the Earth, Cry of the Poor*, 18). That community is always available to me, beckoning me, and its beauty, mystery, and harmony can be my sacred text.[209]

This is a description of the ritual's fullness! These small ritual gestures can help, perhaps, only perhaps, to build community organizations, joining those already in place to bring together the ecological, the social, the cultural, the economic, the multispecies, and the planetary layers of our collective work. Work that means rethinking the common good, or as Stengers describes it, the work of hesitation, where no single account is central. Instead, our collective efforts blossom out into new forms of living, bringing together newly discovered agent beings, humans, and more-than humans, even spirits and ghosts, to shape a cosmos that "refers to the unknown constituted by [the] multiple, divergent worlds and to the articulations of which they could eventually be capable."[210]

We can start by walking within the patch of land in which we find ourselves, paying attention, checking in on and celebrating all that lives there, registering our losses, counting our dead, mourning every being now departed. Paying attention, we inventory our history, so that our past can guide us, now and into the future. Walking, we register what is in need of transformation, regeneration, healing, and metamorphosis. Walking, we respond to emergencies that demand our care and protect and give space to what is emerging, to continue to grow.

Even this simple practice, though, won't come without struggle, problems, violence, and great destruction. We will be confronted with denial, exhaustion, and with so-called inevitable choices that will always bend toward development and growth. We will indeed romanticize our efforts and believe we have all the answers. It will take a while for us all to understand the processes of life and death, creation and destruction, the proper scale of things, the entities around, the potentialities and dangers of everything, the time, systems and patterns of things, the energies of each place and relation, and the entropy of it all. We will protect what doesn't need protection; we will anthropomorphize nonhuman behavior for the sake of our own understanding. It will take a long time to let go of our conviction that humans are the center of the world. And this release will not come without a painful reorientation of our lifestyles, desires, and received knowledge.

Over time and space, though, paying attention to the space around me, I will be able to rise and be grateful for the air we breathe, feeling in my lungs the vast and fragile nature of the ozone layer above me that allows me to live. Over time, I will bow down to every single being around me, paying attention to and honoring each one. Over time, I will touch the earth, knowing and feeling deeply grateful for what I am made of.

This three-gesture ritual offers a path toward that reconnection, a way of living with the land. Each movement is a form of micropolitics in action. Every time we gaze at the sky, bow to every being, and touch the ground, a molecular revolution is set off, small movements put in motion that can recreate the world. With each gesture, we struggle, we become more compassionate, and learn about ourselves—we reorient our desires. Isn't this what religions are meant to do?

These ritual gestures, then, are both symbolic and effective practical ways of beginning to recreate ourselves and our world, together with those who came before us, those engaged in ritual here and elsewhere, and those who will come after us. Together, we can strengthen each other in this movement and together usher in a new form of living.

CHAPTER TWENTY-ONE

In Theory and in Practice

Our Spiritual Journey

Most of us are probably alike in feeling that we have very little or even no political agency these days. We see and feel the magnitude of multiple disasters and wonder what we can do. It is this sense of helplessness that the ritual I describe in the book is meant to counter, intending to recover a strong sense of political agency. Here, we understand the *political* as having to do not only with party structures and legislation and government, but as an umbrella concept that contains significant aspects of our entire lives: culture, nature, economics, society, race, and class—but also rivers, other species, and the global climate in general. When we talk about the political, we must also recognize that it speaks about deep belonging to a terrain: the idea of a neighborhood expanded to include not only all human beings, but also all of a bioregion's other species and specific weather patterns and atmosphere. Although our current notion of the political doesn't include any of these things, we must recognize that the political is completely dependent upon the ecological. We must also understand that the political system, as we have been used to thinking about it, has been invested in hiding the ecological as unworthy of concern. With this ritual, though, we can and must put the ecological, the patterns of the land, front and center in order to guide and direct the political.

And so this ritual intends to help us create connections with everything that dwells within the land that we call our neighborhood. Whether the result of concentrated thought or spontaneous emergence, these connections can ignite various forms of action in the places we live: can ignite, in other words, molecular revolutions. But again, how can rituals lead to molecular revolutions? Rituals bear within themselves intentions, and the intention of this ritual is to draw our attention, our full perceptions, to the places we live, to all the living beings around us and our landscape within a bioregion. With new perceptions oriented by these intentions, we can start making all sorts of connections, and these connections will be the beginning of a spiritual journey. Our spiritual journey will begin when the new kinship with other beings in the land is established. Perhaps some people will connect with trees, others to opossums, others to birds, others to rivers, others to farming soil, others to bees, and so on. As we become kin, the spirit of the land will make its appearance through the law and the lore of the land.

As discussed before, there is no right way for this ritual to be done, and no proper path to do it. The way each person chooses to engage in it will create a different path that will lead to unexpected forms of relation, perception, concern, and practice. While it possesses a clear orientation and intention, there will always be endless forms of response and relation that will emerge as the ritual is carried out. As we lean in toward our landscapes, those landscapes will also lean toward us, reciprocating our attempts at connection with different responses and perceptions, given the living, varied nature of unique landscapes. The depth of our knowledge about the landscape will determine how we perceive those responses, and the spiritual life that emerges from within this mashup of relations and responses will only grow deeper as the multiple presences found within this regional collective recognize themselves as kin. If the ritual is done collectively, myriad other possibilities will continue to appear.[211]

Anyone, no matter where they are from, no matter the perspectives a particular ZIP code provides, can perform the ritual. There will be immense differences from person/place to person/place in how we do it, what we pay attention to, how we can do things, but everyone can do it. Joerg Rieger continually calls our attention to workers around the world, demanding that we think with them in everything we do, criticizing the way in which poor laborers in particular are so often neglected or dismissed:

> In order to move forward, new materialists and scholars of religion and theology may need to take a step back. When Crockett and Robbins "posit earth as subject" (including "materiality, energy forces, layered strata, atmosphere and magnetosphere, enfolded forms of life"), people who have to work for a living are oddly absent. Yet working people not only make up the majority of humanity; they are also the agents who are sustaining much of human life at present—think not only production and agriculture but also services and care. To be sure, this includes both productive and reproductive labor and contributions to what is considered both material and immaterial (as well as immanent and transcendent).[212]

I come from just such a working-class community; I can truly relate to Rieger's assertions. Paying attention to the poor and the working class is key to wrestling with any issue, especially if we are talking about the earth—so how can this ritual connect to the vulnerable people, those outside of the private business world, those who live in racialized places where the presence of the State is mostly the violence of the police? How can this ritual connect with someone who lives in a neighborhood filled with trees and those who live in food deserts or areas with very little green space, among unpaved roads or concrete jungles crossed every which way by overhead powerlines, surrounded by stray cats and dogs and polluted rivers? Living in a poor neighborhood, you might catch a glimpse of the little weed growing from the sidewalk, or the ants attending to their business; you might recognize your kinship with stray animals or birds while trying to avoid the rats. Inside some homes you will find plants being cared for while in other homes, there is not even food available. Where might we find presences, and where can people find little spots of life where some form of relation can flourish? Places to begin the gestures, forms of life hanging on in hell to be sustained and protected? I remember a neighborhood I visited in a desert village, where there was only one tree and absolutely nothing other than dusty roads. That single tree could be the invitation to build connections with the local area.

That three showed me that any small space/place can be a bioregion. I remember growing up in a place where there were trees strangled by too much cement; my relationship with the land is rooted in my mother singing to the plants she kept inside the house. I remember planting the seeds of a lemon tree in our tiny backyard, and watching as the tree grew happy and strong. I would water and talk to her; that tree was my deepest joy. But when she grew too big to keep in our tiny yard, we had to cut the tree down. I still mourn for that lemon tree.

We can start to make these connections by looking at our own body as a huge ecosystem. Each of us contains around 38 trillion microbial cells and 30 trillion human cells: we are more microbial than human! Each body is a wonder-full bioregion that hosts the same materials as do the stars and the rest of the universe. And wherever we are, our bodies are never alone; we are everywhere and always surrounded by countless other beings. Whether our home is a house or an apartment, millions of microorganisms and other forms of life dwell there alongside us: bacteria, viruses, fungi, spiders, geckos, insects, mice, raccoons, chipmunks, birds, and so on. We share our spaces with water, plants, flowers, and pets. Let some of the fruit in your kitchen start to rot and you will have even more guests in the form of fruit flies. Ecologist Rob R. Dunn tells us that

> Research groups, including my own, began to seriously reconsider the life in our homes. We began to study the life in homes in the way one might inventory a rain forest in Costa Rica or a grassland in South Africa. When we did, we were in for a surprise. We expected to find hundreds of species; instead, we discovered—depending on just how we do the math—upward of two hundred thousand species. Many of these species are microscopic, but others are larger and yet nonetheless overlooked. Breathe in. Inhale deeply. With each breath you bring oxygen deep into

> the alveoli of your lungs, along with hundreds or thousands of species. Sit down. Each place you sit you are surrounded by a floating, leaping, crawling circus of thousands of species. We are never home alone.[213]

This crowded home universe is fascinating. If we are able to walk in wonder with it all, our ritual gestures of rising, bowing, and touching the ground take on much more expanded possibilities of relation and connection. If we pay attention, leaving our homes can lead to the discovery of wonder-full worlds crowded with other living beings and organisms. We can walk through our homes and learn about the insects, worms, plants, flowers, and birds that live there with us. That's exactly what happened to me.

I started paying attention to what was going on outside my window by hanging a bird feeder in my backyard. After a while, chipmunks, squirrels, many kinds of birds, even crows, hawks, owls and vultures, rabbits, and mice started visiting. My Yorkie Amora didn't like any of them, and did her best to chase them away. But they continued to come back, and I started to understand how the ecology of a very small place can grow and support a shared life for many beings, including myself. We also stopped poisoning the grass and everything became so colorful and rich. I turned away from seeing "weeds" as evil presences and welcomed them to our yard. Soon enough we had dandelions, chickweed, crabgrass, creeping Charlie, and others. The bees were so grateful; I watched them dancing around each flower. It reminded me of something Thor Hanson says about privately owned lawns:

> Entomologist and biodiversity crusader Douglas Tallamy calculates that replacing half of the privately owned lawns in North America with native trees, shrubs, and wildflowers would collectively create more than five times the habitat found in Yellowstone and Yosemite National Parks combined. Over forty thousand people have already added their yards to this vision, joining a grassroots campaign that Tallamy calls Homegrown National Park. Dutch ecologist Carijn Beumer has coined an even catchier name for similar efforts to increase urban biodiversity in Europe: BIMBY, short for "biodiversity in my back yard."[214]

I planted sunflowers, and now they return every year! I planted four trees, one of them a cherry blossom tree in honor of the late Peter Perella, the father of my children. This tree is growing so beautifully, surely bringing us Peter's presence in many ways. Although I also recently planted a peach tree and two apple trees, I didn't know how to care for them and they all died. Now I am preparing the ground for new trees to come.

Several flourishing urban movements are attempting to transform impoverished neighborhoods through new ways of caring for the environment. For example, the Alliance to Reforest the Amazon is dedicated to reforesting the cleared territories of traditional local peoples.[215] And individual neighborhoods and cities find their own ways to restore or maintain their bioregion. Regular people around the world are coming together to take care of trees, fight deforestation, and maintain bodies of water.[216] A group near my own home works to protect our local rivers.[217] Entire countries are getting involved in the efforts. "As of 2019, China provided multiple forms of support to small farmers, in order both to help them implement improved agricultural practices and to encourage reforestation." Costa Rica used "taxes on fossil fuels and fees covered by major water users, such as hydroelectric power plants and sanitation and industrial concerns," to fund ecosystem restoration. South Korea has undertaken efforts at reforesting areas degraded by war and other developments. Niger has seen "a spontaneous movement by farmers themselves to reverse" desertification due to French colonial agricultural practices. "With the support of NGOs, the community began to change the landscape through the use of agroforestry techniques. This is how an area of around 5 million hectares was recovered by associating agricultural production with tree planting."[218] The United Nations has also launched its Decade of Ecosystem Restoration. Between 2021 and 2030, the organization will work with nineteen cities around the globe on projects of ecological restoration.[219] A specific ecosystem and landscape will be restored in each city.

From small stories throughout the small ecosystems around us, we can expand our attention to and care for a larger bioregion. For me, practicing the three gestures I've been describing changed me, bringing me to a greater sense of belonging to the land. For example, I befriended a tree at Adams-Ricci Community Park, near my home in Enola, Pennsylvania. I called her Wonder; I often visit and talk to her, and so many times, she has returned the favor of caring for me. At some point in our years-long conversation, I realized she was sick. After doing some research and learning there was nothing I could do to cure her illness, I began praying for her when I visited, and I still do. Through this connection I realized that Conodoguinet Creek, which runs past Wonder, is a tributary of the Susquehanna River—which is perhaps the oldest river in the world.

This knowledge changed my entire relationship with my bioregion; here I am, living so close to one of the most ancient entities on earth, a river that has supported and been supported by the Susquehannock People, with an amazing history! But that history, filled with colonial destruction, abuse and destruction, also broke my heart, and pushed me to join with others in caring for the river and one of its nearby tributaries, working to prevent industries from polluting the waters. Now I visit the Susquehanna to listen to it, to see and feel its presence, to sustain the spiritual relationship I have established with this ancient entity. It is an entire ecosystem that requires constant care and attention to the movement and presence of other species, beings, and spirit/Spirit/s. If my practice of the three-gesture ritual has resulted in these changes, I believe those gestures and transformations can become bolder still, especially as people continue to come together and demand policies and accountability that will support what still remains of my bioregion.

Beyond my personal experience, though, my students have also felt the difference made by practicing this ritual. Every day during the semester, students are required to do the gestures I've described and write a journal entry, or meditation, about how the ritual has influenced their interaction with the environment. The students come from various religious traditions and also none. Their reflections below demonstrate careful examination of the practice of the ritual and how these gestures may be used by people of many religious and non-religious traditions. We start with Safiya Rebhi, who shows how she understood the ritual interacting with her Muslim religious practices.

> My body usually enters the ritual carrying its own accumulation of faith, memory, and lived experience. The movements of salah—standing, bowing, prostrating, and sitting—are not merely a composition of gestures but embodied acts of submission and Dhikr remembrance. Their internal experience is profoundly personal, shaped by my relationship to my tradition within an American context . . .. Practicing the gestures of rising, bowing, and prostration in a public park, Riverside Park in New York City, as a living assemblage of soil, trees, wind, birds, and human presence, rather than within a designated prayer space, reframes Islamic embodied prayer as an explicitly ecological and relational act.
>
> Standing among trees and beneath an open sky intensifies the experience of qiyam as accountability within creation rather than apart from it. The Qur'anic verses recited while standing no longer feel abstract or distant; they circulate through the air shared with leaves, insects, and other bodies, underscoring the Qur'anic claim that all created beings glorify God in ways humans may not comprehend.
>
> Rising here becomes an acknowledgment that revelation is addressed not only to the individual worshiper but to humanity as both accountable and part of our falling ecological systems.
>
> Bowing in this space sharpens the ethical dimensions of ruku (the bowing). The act of bending the body while surrounded by grass, uneven ground, and visible signs of growth and decay renders humility unmistakably material. In this posture, grief is no longer metaphorical; it is grounded in the recognition of trampled soil, polluted air, and the histories of displacement and enclosure that shape even cultivated green spaces. Bowing thus becomes a site of moral inventory, where gratitude for life's abundance coexists with mourning for what has been damaged or rendered invisible. The park, often perceived as a neutral or restorative space, reveals itself as politically and ecologically contested, demanding from us not passive appreciation but ethical attentiveness.
>
> Prostration in the park intensifies the theological force of sujud (to touch). Placing the forehead directly upon the earth collapses any illusion of human separation from the ground that sustains and will eventually receive the body. While Islamic theology resists attributing spiritual

agency to the earth itself, this posture affirms the earth as a divinely created witness to human conduct. The texture, temperature, and resistance of the ground interrupt abstraction, re-centering humility as an embodied truth rather than a moral ideal. In this moment, remembrance of ancestors, laborers, and displaced peoples becomes inseparable from the land beneath the body, emphasizing that history, ecology, and worship are intertwined.

Practiced in the park, this ritual enactment amplifies the processes of inventory, transformation, and emergence already present within Islamic prayer. The environment functions as a mirror and a demand, exposing the gap between ritual devotion and lived responsibility. Prayer here does not resolve ecological crises but sharpens awareness of it, insisting that worship must extend beyond the mat into modes of care, restraint, and justice . . . prayer [is] not as a retreat from the world, but as a disciplined return to it—one that binds devotion to God with ethical obligation toward the earth and all who inhabit it.[220]

Melanie Baker offered the following thoughts:

This week, *To Rise, To Bow, To Land* became a gesture of gratitude and reciprocity. Influenced by Kimmerer's *The Serviceberry*, I began to notice how this practice quietly echoes the principles of a gift economy.[221] In rising, I receive the breath of the morning as a gift. In bowing, I acknowledge the source of that gift—the earth, the Creator, the web of life. And in landing, I am called not to hoard the peace I feel, but to offer it outward: in presence, in kindness, in attention. The spiritual discipline took on the quality of a "sacrament of enoughness" and a daily reorientation toward abundance. Kimmerer teaches that gratitude is the first response to receiving a gift, and reciprocity the second. I see this practice not only as a private prayer but as a gesture of participation in a sacred cycle. It's an embodied resistance to the capitalist drive for accumulation.[222]

Lawyer Melissa Bellew wrote in one of her meditations:

I traveled to Kentucky this week. Returning to my birthplace and my beloved Appalachia stir much emotion. I targeted this visit to trudge to the Little Sandy Riverbank on the border of my parents' farm on the unceded land of the Shawnee. I am focusing my final project in this class upon the river and the rituals that surround this river's survival and personhood. This focus permitted me the opportunity to perform this gesture practice near the riverbank, as the raging flood waters prohibited riverbank access. I performed the gesture at the river twice during my weekend visit. The emotion rocked me. Placing my forehead on the cold, damp ground near the river brought me to tears. I felt truly the

> power of my childhood and life on that farm and river surge into me. "To the ground I touch" never held such power for me in the time that this gesture practice has enveloped me in September, 2024. This practice has heightened my earth connection. Repeatedly touching the ground, or water, has pulsed with power and yearning. I feel a need to protect the land and water deep within me and this gesture practice's simplicity has permitted my focus to remain on the touching of the land or water.[223]

Another student offered the following:

> The moment that I raised my arms to the skies, inhaled the fresh, damp air, dug my toes into the dirt, cast my eyes to the clouds, and opened my mouth to let loose a joyous prayer, I felt free—freer than I've felt in a long time. Every cell within me seemed to leap with gratitude and shout: *Finally! You're here!* I then bowed to the trees, the birds, and the squirrels, and lowered myself all the way to the ground, letting the wet dew seep into my pants and shirt. As I inhaled the smell of dirt and worms, I realized that I was finally paying attention to what it means to be alive. The metamorphosis that I experienced with my face in the grass felt like magic. In the words of Tom Driver: "There is something healthy about ritual's assumption that human reality is essentially dramatic, that at bottom life is not something to be *treated*, as scientifically based medicine treats disease, but something to be *enacted*, as in the enactment of one's own being in the world or the enactment of a cure."[224] In my own backyard, I was enacting my freedom by stepping outside my walls and connecting, literally, with Mother Earth. By connecting, I was finally paying attention.

Another meditation from a Buddhist student:

> Throughout this week, I have found immense kinship with the trees outside my window. I have noticed which branches the squirrels tend to frequent, and the ways in which the leaves "breathe" throughout the day. In the morning crisp, a little wilted in midday sun, and again something more vibrant after a storm. They have always been there with me but I have not always welcomed them onto my meditation mat. To rise is to extend my arms up to the sky as they do, because I am also alive! What joy in this effort to reach towards what is not yet within grasp and to still be rooted to the earth, growing in all directions towards the living and the dying.
>
> While bowing, I found myself thinking of my grandmother's grace. Her prayer beads and rosaries know something of the rhythm and routine of prayer that mimics the death and resurrection of Jesus. To feel it barbed and in the body, to succumb to the limits and grandeur of a human life. In bowing, I also bring newness to the bows to the three

jewels of Buddha, Dharma, and Sangha. I bow in reverence, in aspiration, and in community with all who are bowing and between.

In the prostration, there is something returning to the ground. Being rooted. I continue to discover aspects of my Christian upbringing that are nourishing. I continue to reintegrate ideas and practices into a new context. Prayer is something I do as a Buddhist, though it sometimes has different names. I need not be afraid of this word or practice. The vessel has been shattered and returned to the earth. What emerges again after the prostration is a return to living, a start to acting and closing the gap between our prayer and our living. This is a beautiful baptism to begin anew, to start with a beginner's mind, to greet the moment as urgent and vital, and to remember our interconnectedness.[225]

CHAPTER TWENTY-TWO

Flaco, a Molecular Revolution

Stories reveal what theory explains. Theory illuminates and stories teach us how to live. Let me share the story of Flaco, a Eurasian eagle-owl who lived in New York's Central Park,[226] whose brief life and death became a molecular revolution—a small event that transformed thousands of people's relationships with urban wildlife and revealed the power of attention, care, and collective mourning. This story shows us what our three gestures aim to create: connections that move us from prayer to action, from individual practice to collective transformation.

As mentioned before, the Earth has their own ways of showing us discontent and nonacceptance of the ways we live. In fact, the Earth often holds up a mirror to us, one that we seem unwilling to see. Covid was one of the Earth's clear signs of how misguided we are, destroying other species' habitats and dismantling necessary boundaries between species and landscapes. Not just signs of our disconnection from the Earth, but also, perhaps, a call for a new awareness, a conversion, a metamorphosis, a new way of thinking-feeling-doing-living. Sometimes, these signs lead to transformation, even if ephemeral.

Flaco is such an example.[227] The Eurasian eagle-owl was born in captivity in North Carolina in 2010 and was moved to New York City's Central Park Zoo, where he lived until 2023. One day, through an act of what some have called vandalism, and I call liberation, someone opened Flaco's cage, and he escaped the zoo to live freely. At first, the zoo tried to capture him; they were concerned he wouldn't survive in the wild. But contrary to expectations, Flaco was able to fend for himself and live well for a full year. He flew around Manhattan, visiting several neighborhoods, apartment buildings, and windows, feeding on rats and pigeons. It seems he lived a full life! But on February 24, 2024, Flaco was pronounced dead, having ingested four different types of rat poison and suffering from herpes contracted from a pigeon. The toxins in his body may have caused Flaco to pass out while flying, and when he hit a building, he died.

Flaco's short year of life outside the zoo gave rise to changes in the city and the state of New York. While he was free, people wandered the city trying to find the owl and take pictures. They started paying attention to his habits, trying to listen to his calls and finding joy in their search for him. Flaco, a Spanish name that means *skinny*, became not only a symbol of the city and a sort of metaphor; for many people, he became a real bird, relating to him in many ways. Since his species was originally from Europe, Asia, and parts of North Africa, he was seen as an immigrant or a refugee trying to survive and thrive far from home in New York City. He was the only Eurasian eagle-owl to have lived freely in the United States.

New York City-based writer and photographer Jonathan Hollinsworth says that "the individual who cut a hole in Flaco's Central Park enclosure released two Flacos into the world. The first was the living, breathing Eurasian Eagle-Owl of Manhattan, un-taming himself before our eyes . . . . While we tragically lost the real, singular Flaco, the Flaco of our dreams and imaginations is very much alive."[228] With Flaco free, we could project our own freedom onto him. Our anthropomorphic projections had us viewing him as an immigrant, a symbol of freedom and the wonderful feeling of possessing that freedom. But we also saw Flaco as a lone soul searching for a partner in a city where so many of its residents also feel lonely. Hearing Flaco hooting for hours in search of a mate, we felt our own longing for someone to share our lives.

Flaco didn't just help us see ourselves; he also led us to learn about the unique ways owls live, interact, eat, love, feel. People may even have come to realize that a long-eared owl, for example, would perceive the world very differently than Flaco, who allowed us the possibility of growing closer to another being with its particular habits and needs. The free-flying owl drew both adults' and children's attention to the wildlife living in a city of concrete and steel, an area containing over a million buildings[229]—into which about 250,000 birds crash annually, and which, with all the light they emit causing disorientation, alter birds' migration patterns.[230] Even if only briefly, what Flaco may have been able to show residents of New York was the lack of separation between nature and the city, since every city *is* part of nature, and every species is a full inhabitant of the city.

Wherever we live, it *is* nature. Culture is a way of arranging nature, and nature is the earth, air, fire, and water that come with every culture. In the space where I am writing now, everything is nature: the computer I'm using to type, the books I read, the cup of coffee or tea I'm drinking, the clothes I'm wearing and the beads and necklaces on my body, the house in which it's all located, the window looking outside—everything is nature, including me. All of us are part of what we call nature, part of the planet.

But Flaco also showed us how terribly we relate to and interact with other species. The fact that rodents are filled with poison shows that we don't know how to handle the presence of rats and mice. And since most of their diet consists of rats, every raptor in New York City is also ingesting that poison.

Flaco offered us layers of awareness: about the vastness of other species' lives in the city. For example, we could name the rats and doves in virtually any city as symbols of new ways of living, surviving, and becoming with humans. Fahim Amir mentions the pigeons:

> The pigeon is a living metaphor for excess and communication, for insubordinate migration without a fatherland, and for producing solidarity in improbable places. The pigeon is a cipher for wealth, proliferation, and sociality ("pigeons fly to where pigeons are"). It is based in material, non-innocent history and the associated multifarious production of meaning. But the pigeon is also just as much a sign of excess and of the utopian[231]

Flaco's layers of awareness continue: awareness the troubling practice of keeping animals in cages; about our lack of attention to species living right beside us; about the ways we often feel threatened by other species; about the need to be more careful, gentler, more willing to embrace other species; about the need to make space for other species and honor and care for them; about how distanced we are from the full life of our cities; about the fact that we are "guardians" of the places we live; about so much more. [232]

Flaco became a force to reckon with; he brought New York City to a halt, and his presence rippled across the world. Because Flaco's favorite tree was a particular oak, people turned it into a sacred place. Artists honored Flaco, painting murals and portraits and writing poetry; children made drawings for and wrote letters to him; books and music were written about him; *The New York Times* placed the announcement of his death at the center of its first page; and the New York Historical Society Museum and Library created an entire exhibition about him. Even more powerfully, all of these feelings and gestures led to new laws. In 2024, the New York Statewide Bird Safe Buildings Act in New York was renamed the FLACO Act: *Feathered Lives Also Count Act*, which outlined new efforts to care for birds and means of controlling the rat population.[233]

Perhaps Flaco was indeed a molecular revolution, one that ignited countless responses across the city and the state.[234] Even though his moment was brief in a city that never sleeps, Flaco reminded us all of how much we still yearn to connect with the land; he recalled to us a part of ourselves we'd lost along the way. What the Eurasian eagle-owl showed us is that, as was true for him, animals around the world are losing their own habitats and attempting to adapt to urban life. Coyotes are showing up in San Francisco and capybaras are making their homes in the cities of South America. They are demanding we pay attention, that we realize we are not the only ones living on this planet.[235]

Marrianne DeMarco, a New York resident, said, 'It is a little like the end of . . .' she paused . . . 'the end of a dream that we were all hoping to hold on to.'"[236] Perhaps these gestures can allow the dream to continue, joining people around the planet, helping us to connect with, protect, and live together with the land and other species. The ritual offered here is intended to be part of these efforts. If we practice them deliberately, we may rediscover a new-old earth, and our shared future may even last a little longer.

CHAPTER TWENTY-THREE

The Power of Ritualized Gestures

Right now, it seems the arc of the moral universe is bending toward extinction. Unless we change in both small and large ways our current mode of living, our future will contain no possibility of full existence, or even, perhaps, of survival.

We know we have to start somewhere—but we also don't know where. Let us at least begin with a gesture where we are and discover and foster new means of connection, feed new desires, and find alternative ways of living. While we rise, bow, and prostrate locally, we resist the machinery of death; we denounce the concentration of wealth in the hands of a few individuals; we fight to stop fossil-fuel capitalism, the fixity of nation-states, the end of liberal democracy, growing fascism, white supremacy and racial oppression, exploitative agribusiness, invasive high-tech industries, and combative military powers. It is easy to understand all these correlations through the notion of the *petrosexoracial regime*, as defined by Paul B. Preciado:

> The petrosexoracial regime is a more of a social organization and a set of technologies of government and representation that developed from the fifteenth century onwards with the expansion of colonial capitalism and the extension of racial and sexual epistemologies from Europe to the entire planet.[237]

The vastness of this petrosexoracial regime feels overwhelming, invading even our most intimate thoughts. Rituals, though, can counteract this weight and lead us to new forms of practice and agency. They help us reenvision the past so that a better future will be possible; the particular ritual I propose in this book allows us to access and learn from modes of being that were present before the imposition of world-spanning religions: regional forms of thinking locally along with the land and the spirits it hosts.

Even when carried out by a "lone" individual, the gestures I've been describing are made with the collective in mind, beginning in a neighborhood and aiming at the universal. This small ritual binds together bodies, territories, and worlds, helping us think about, imagine, fabulate, and bring into being alternative forms of not only personal relations but also governance and means of production. The intention is not the return to an ideal place and time but the creation of communities that, even if they seem to have nothing in common, learn to live together. We build upon the new insights we receive from ritual; we expand upon them, let them show us what is possible, what is urgent, and what is necessary in a given place. And we combine those new insights with past and present wisdom, practices, and knowledge: a bricolage of worlds interacting for the wellbeing of our present and our future. Nothing short of an entirely new mode of life will do. New desires! New dreaming! A new unconscious!

*

Again, practicing this ritual can feel very idealistic. Its gestures, though, can act as glowing embers beneath the ashes our civilization has left behind. It will help us invent new political forms, transcending the politics we know—free from the power of capital or the state, free to pay attention to extra-modern ontologies and create new forms of perception, subjectivity, animism, and ways of life. This ritual reminds us that some other way of life is possible, with and/or without religious systems—providing us a vision of action and imagination we so desperately need.

So when I rise, I rise to resist damaging lifestyles, breaking free from oppressive forms of living and inventing new practices. When I rise, I confront policies that lead to human, animal, and ecological death. Gazing toward the threatened ozone layer, I listen for lessons about the climate crisis that are blowing in the wind. I commit to the seasons, to the law and lore of the land and every living being around me!

When I bow, I move in service to those who have come before us, to those who are living near me. When I bow, I commit to honoring all who struggle to live in the midst of so much destruction; to mourning those who are dying; to caring for all species: humans and other animals, trees, plants, insects, rivers, birds, vegetation, mountains, forests, oceans, . . . I commit to the seasons, to the law and lore of the land and every living being around me!

When I prostrate myself, I connect to the place I now belong and vow to care for the soil, to care for the seeds. When I prostrate myself, I pledge to fight against the forces extracting fossils from the earth, privatizing land and seeds, and treating the land as a source of profit. When I prostrate myself,

I vow to honor all species, humans and more than humans, around me. I commit to the seasons, to the law and lore to the seasons, to the law and lore of the land and every living being around me!

This ritual erases the boundaries between material and symbolic life: in other words, it denies the separation between matters of economy and the freedoms found within and among individuals and societies, between profit flows and the collective interpretation, negotiation, and disputation about our daily lived experiences. Ritual works in us at the molecular, pre-boundary level in order to change the universe. It leads us to the deep conviction that we can no longer accept the current status quo; it leads to the appearance of new ways of living. Perhaps already latent within us, these bodily gestures may help bring to light and even to fruition these new possibilities.

*

In the end, every gesture is the container of a story, of a thousand stories, stories of each other that are both the same and different each time they are told, stories that can save us and stories that reveal how our lifestyles result in catastrophe and remove from us the ability to analyze, think and feel about, and engage the world. Our habits and practices tell a story of our lives together, of the Spirit and the spirits who live in us. Ritual gestures weave a tale that shows us how we can cast out the demons within us and free ourselves—and ourselves as a collective of many species. The story points the way to the freedom of all beings, of their transformation into forms, not of enclosure but of relationality and connectivity. Ancient ritual forms of wisdom are connected to new ways of living.

And we need a spiritual revolution to bring in these new ways. One that is led by the law of nature, meaning the ways of the earth, the needs, the offerings, and the demands of the land. *Lex natura* before all else![238] From that law we are able to care for each other and all beings.

Along with the Psalmist, we must sit down and weep by our rivers.[239] We must bow at the banks of dead and dying rivers and weep with them, mourning their passing. Hear the waters' sounds; note what they are saying. When you stand back up, rise in glory for this river's fierceness in struggling against constant attacks and violence and destruction. Listen to all of the sounds around you. The sounds of the birds, of the trees. Look for any riparian vegetation that may be protecting the river. Honor and care for them! Then prostrate yourself: put your head on the ground and honor the lives of the rivers who have given us so much. Listen for subterranean rivers, worms moving underground, the fungi, and the earth pulsing. Remember humus, humility! Consciously offer deep respect to the place—and then continue out into the world carrying these sensations and sounds within you, feeling the connection to all beings and assuming responsibility for their lives. Connect with your neighbors and ask them to do the ritual with you. Lead them in this prayer. Be led by them in this prayer. Learn the prayers of the wind, of the rivers and the mountains, of the fire, the trees, the worms, and the soil, the opossums, raccoons, capybaras and jaguars, crows, hummingbirds, and the fireflies. Then together, demand that politicians learn these prayers as well so that they can care for the rivers, demand that they shutter polluters, and bring the rivers once again to life!

Do the same thing if you live near the ocean. Go to the shore, face the waters, and bow to the ocean in gratitude. Pause and listen to the waves. Rise up in wonder at the ocean's immensity, its history and inhabitants, the home it offers for billions of other beings. If you are able, walk into the water; submerge yourself, and listen to the sounds beneath the surface. Back on shore, bow down, mourning the ocean's ongoing death, its being starved of oxygen, its suffering extreme heat and acidification.[240] Pray for the of the ocean, the plankton, and all species living there. Learn their prayers. Remember humus, humility! Consciously offer deep respect to the place. Then prostrate yourself: put your forehead on the sand and connect to it and everything around it, feeling that you are also part of the ocean. Pay attention and listen to the species feeding along the shore—crabs, barnacles, starfish, anemones, shorebirds, and small fish—on the food the waves have brought them. Be grateful to the tide pools and their ecosystems. Say a prayer of gratitude for all life inside the ocean; pray that the ocean may continue to support our very lives. Then leave the place and join with others in trying to save the oceans.

If you live in an area where fossil fuel extraction is occurring, go as close as you can to the scene of uprooting and put your head to the ground. Millions of beings who died before us have turned to soil, to shale, to materials holding the ground in place for us. Honor them, thank them. Listen to the land, hear its cries and cry with the earth. Remember humus, humility! Consciously offer deep respect to the place. Be thankful for all who have come before you. Remember that the soil is alive thanks to so many beings: microorganisms, dead plants, bones, water, ants, insects, insect larvae, seeds, crustaceans, spiders, and millipedes. Remember that birds find food beneath the soil. Then bow, mourning the destruction involved in this rich world being turned to fuel and upsetting earth's planetary balance. Then rise in gratitude for everyone trying to hold the world together. Go into the world and learn how fossil fuels are at the core of our environmental crises, how much the fossil fuel industry profits from their destruction. Join with those around you to speak against politicians supporting the industry, to insist that this extraction and devastation be brought to an end.

If you live in a city, walk through the streets and bow to the people and the animals that you see. Bow down to the trees you pass by and thank them for the home they give to so many beings. Mourn the death of so many people we have abandoned and displaced, and the trees cut down to make room for concrete. Say glory for each flower coming out of the concrete resisting, reminding us of our potencies! Raise your eyes to the clouds and thank the people who are there and the trees for the rain we receive. Remember that animals who survive in cities are signs of strength and courage and adaptation; recognize that they are showing us how to survive in our own world! Remember how the poor and the homeless show us the absurd ways we have organized our societies. When you see a homeless person, do something: offer food, money, perhaps shelter somewhere in the city. When you find a patch of dirt, put your feet on it, with or without shoes, and thank it for the life it is giving to us. Remember humus, humility! Listen to everything around you. If you can't hear any birds, you are in danger. Listen to the cries of the poor. Collect every sound you hear and pray with them all. As you walk through the city, remember that everything is nature; you don't need to leave built-up areas to know that nature is there, that nature is everywhere we step, that nature is everything we wear, that nature is us.

Practicing this ritual provides an indication of how and what we want our society to be. We rise and we say we cannot live in a world unchanged. Take strength with each prayer, remembering that every life-form possesses agency and ways of adapting and surviving. Fight with each prayer against all forms of death, for this struggle is exactly what these liturgical gestures are all about: making connections, and mourning and resurrecting the dead!

As we perform this ritual, though, we must pause and be still. We must allow ourselves the time to do nothing but sit next to a tree or a river and contemplate, listen, dwell. Praying in this way will bring us to accept that we don't know what to do, and still we must wait. It will bring us to embrace the paradox of poets and fighters living together, each reminding the other of what is important. While the first say poetry is all we need to create a new world, the revolutionary counters that we have too many poets, and that we will continue to lose what we have if there are no fighters to transform the world. The poet agrees that fighters are needed—but that revolution that sacrifices everything else as it goes forward will only exhaust you, and quickly, just as the powers-that-be would have it: rushing headlong into war to die as fast as possible. After a long discussion, each reminds the other of what poet-guerrilla warrior Che Guevara said: "hay que endurecerse pero sin perder la ternura jamás": you must endure without ever losing your tenderness.

As we continue to make these ritual gestures, we must hold onto the unflinching belief that we can turn our catastrophic conditions around. We need what African American writer Octavia E. Butler called prodigy:

> Prodigy is, in its essence, adaptability and persistent, positive obsession. Without persistence, what remains is an enthusiasm of the moment. Without adaptability, what remains may be channeled into destructive fanaticism. Without positive obsession, there is nothing at all.[241]

Perhaps our ritual gestures will help us develop prodigy within us. To adapt is not to get used to forms of death; it is instead to learn how to invent new, postcapitalist forms of life, in tune with the earth. We must persist in our fight against fascism, extractivism, and the destruction of all beings on this planet. But doing that will require spiritual discipline. It is not going to be easy. Spiritual discipline entails sacrifice in the sense of making life as a whole holy—giving ourselves to others, to live collectively and not as isolated individuals.

This kind of persistent, daily spiritual practice—I saw it first in my mother. Almost every day of her life, she has sung hymns to the plants—but it wasn't until I turned fifty that I paid attention to her singing. Visiting her one day, I finally noticed, as I hadn't seen before what she was doing. As a young displaced person, she had worked on another person's land. Now the plants—her plants—are her territory, the continuation of her body. When I feel overwhelmed by current catastrophes, I remember my mother persistently singing to the plants. Her daily ritual recalls and enacts a faithful discipline that I want to mimic; I want to take refuge in the tender revolutionary act of that singing, in singing to my own plants, in singing to my people, in singing to my bioregion.

These spiritual gestures, our own songs, can counter that first gesture made by the Portuguese in Brazil, the act of murder still being repeated. Our positive obsession must be *to rise* as warriors, fighting every agent of death on our planet. Our positive obsession must be *to bow* to every living being, having compassion for all who suffer and mourning all who have died. Our positive obsession must be *to prostrate* ourselves and discover the depths of who we are: humus, humility, strength, honor, decency, fortitude, soil, water, wind, and fire. But to do these gestures, we must recognize our needs of and for each other. Or as Anna Lowenhaupt Tsing says, "staying alive—for every species—requires livable collaborations. Collaboration means working across difference, which leads to contamination. Without collaborations, we all die."[242]

FIGURE 7 *Integration.*

Conclusion

Pay Attention and Tell a Story

Let me end with a story that captures everything this book is about: how paying attention to the smallest beings can transform even the most desperate circumstances. During a workshop, Martinha, a woman who worked in a detention center in Brazil, told me the following story. One day, the inmates were fighting. When she went to find out what was going on, one of the men said, "He stole my baby! He stole my baby!" She didn't understand; the inmates weren't allowed to have outside visitors. As she came closer, though, she realized the men were talking about the babies a spider had just given birth to; the fight was over who would be responsible for the spider family. Martinha said that there were enough babies for everyone, that they had to be careful with the mother spider, and that they shouldn't take her newborns from her. Each person was assigned a baby to care for, and the inmates now had a purpose: they were taking care of the spiders, keeping predators away and giving the newborns space to grow. They were careful to make sure the mother was able to build a web that would let her catch enough food for her family.

Here we have both the tragedy and the beauty of human ingenuity. On the one hand, we see humans locked behind bars, forgotten. The rest of society fears them, and no one wants them in their community. The general consensus seems that it would be best if they died in prison. It's unsurprising that the inmates would identify with those spiders, which instill the same disgust and fear in most humans that the incarcerated do; so many of us, as soon as we see spiders, try to kill them, even knowing that not all of them are remotely dangerous to human beings. So in this prison we see two forms of life that have been pushed aside, viewed as hazards to everyone else. Here, though, both were able to connect with each other. Thanks to the spiders, the inmates discovered a sense of freedom and purpose they longed for. In turn, the inmates not only refrained from stomping on the spiders; they cared for and even loved them. A web of relationship and connection formed between the two species, the matriarch in her material web becoming mother to them all. As romanticized as this story sounds, it also reveals the possibility of creating unexpected relationships and forms of care. From creatures to be feared or despised, the spiders were transformed into beings to be cherished and protected.

If we allow ourselves to learn from those inmates, we too could create a world of interspecies relations inherently defined by mutual care. This book is perhaps an attempt to do exactly what those inmates did: pay attention, be aware, craft a story, and care for every being that surrounds us. Perhaps the ritual described here aims at nothing more than helping us find our own silence, our own quietness—and within it, the realization that we do have space within us to allow other beings to be full parts of our very short lives and add their beauty to them.

*

We began this book with a tree—the first tree cut down by Portuguese colonizers in 1500 to make a cross, the first liturgical gesture of the colonial era that would kill fifty-six million Indigenous people and devastate the land. That gesture of extraction has been repeated for five hundred years: cutting, mining, drilling, taking, and destroying. It became the gesture that shaped modernity itself, the movement that created capitalism's insatiable appetite. But gestures can be replaced. The inmates caring for spiders show us how: through attention, through care, and through the daily practice of bowing to life instead of destroying it. Our three gestures—rising to acknowledge the sky and all that gives us breath, bowing to every being around us, and prostrating to touch the earth in humility—these are the counter-gestures to that first act of colonial violence.

Where the Portuguese cut down a tree to claim dominion, we touch the ground to remember we are humus, soil, earth. Where they extracted to possess, we bow to belong. Where they rose to conquer, we rise to give thanks. Every time we practice these gestures, we participate in undoing that 500-year-old ritual of death. Every time we bow to a tree instead of cutting it down, we practice the spiritual discipline of life. This is our positive obsession: to replace the gesture of extraction with the gesture of relation, to counter five centuries of taking with the daily practice of returning, of touching the earth and saying, "I belong to you. Teach me how to live."

I think it is only fitting to finish this book with a prayer from Osage scholar George E. "Tink" Tinker:

> wakonda monshita! wakonda uidseta! witzigoe ski ikoe! winachnon minkshe.
> Grandmother! Grandfather! Sacred One Above and Sacred One Below.
> Thank you for this day, for life itself,
> and especially for this gathering of relatives in the struggle for liberation.[243]

AFTERWORD

"Going Forth with Hope and Determination"

Bonnie J. Miller-McLemore

Reader beware. You cannot read this book and go unchanged. This book will shake your foundations and liberate you to see another way forward during one of the toughest periods in human and earth history. You *can* make a difference. This book will inspire you to do so.

It is an honor and a challenge to offer a few afterwords. How can I do justice to the rich prose offered herein? The gracious invitation to add an afterword came in the season of Advent 2025. Frankly, it has been a grueling political year, especially if you care about trees or water or birds or animals or insects or air, and more so if your life has been directly impacted by current governmental policies on any number of fronts—health care, immigration, education, human rights, *and*, of course, *climate*. Not a day has passed in 2025 without another nauseating, infuriating statement or action by the current US president and his loyal followers and implementors. Many environmental actions seem based on sheer malice and spite, like removing all the electric vehicle chargers from a local federal building or changing the name of the National Renewable Energy Laboratory in Colorado, decreed the National Laboratory of the Rockies on December 1, dropping "renewable." Is "renewable" now a dirty word? Worse yet are actions aimed at inciting fear and generating despair, like deploying the National Guard to major cities to protect ICE agents and promoting fossil fuels, thereby reversing progress on cooling our climate at a time when we don't have time to regress.

It didn't help that alongside Cláudio's book, I was also reading *Is a River Alive?* by well-known British nature writer Robert Macfarlane, a book that despite its many hopeful notes reminded me again and again of the myriad ways Western capitalism and "development" has polluted, diverted, cemented over, dammed, drained, and murdered our rivers. Once more, we humans have shit on the gifts of the earth. We built cities by rivers to survive and then "confined" and "imprisoned" them in drains and tunnels to such an extent that most urban peoples today don't even know such waters exist, "their voices . . . heard at street level, if at all, as whispers drifting from manhole covers or drain grills" as Macfarlane puts it (16–17).

And then, in the third week of Advent, the lights in my home went out. Literally. Ninety-to-hundred-mile-per-hour winds led Xcel Energy to shut down power to thousands of customers on Colorado's Front Range to prevent the spread of fires from fallen electric lines. A big "weather event," they said. We joined thousands of people without power for five or more days. Living without power, and hence without lights, heat, water, cooking, toilets, cell and internet service, was a powerful reminder of just how dependent I—and we humans—have become on modern conveniences, many of which depend on the burning of the very fossil fuels that have, in a vicious circle, contributed to such catastrophic "events." In contrast to only a few decades ago, you cannot experience extreme weather today without the deadly drumbeat of climate destruction beating hauntingly in the background.

It is easy to throw up our hands in despair. What can anyone do?

Cláudio, in his amazing wisdom and courage, invites us to *gesture otherwise*. He begins with his conversion story, a moment when he felt a call to respond to the cries of the earth, recognizing in Robin Wall Kimmerer's mandate to forge ceremonies to mourn and celebrate the earth his own incredible gifts for ritual craft and artistry. And so, he went to work.

Cláudio invites us into a threefold ritual, joining ourselves through bodily action to the earthlings around us, *rising* to praise, *bowing* to acknowledge and honor, and *prostrating* our bodies to release and reconnect with the earth. Rise, bow, prostrate. Repeat. Do these acts every day, even several times a day, and you will be changed. And the change that you perform will become a spark alongside others to make a difference in seeing the planet and its life forms anew and acting accordingly on the earth's behalf.

Immersed in a broad array of literature, Cláudio also offers a goldmine of mandatory reading if people really desire authentic relationship and reciprocity with the earth, especially those practical, liberation, and ecological theologians who profess connection to material religion and realities. He pushes practical, liberation, and ecological theology one step further, overhauling and reinvigorating our common definitions of "context" and "location," insisting that these concepts must consider qualities and pragmatic actions often ignored and pushed aside. Just take an inventory of "the places [you] inhabit so that [you] can learn with those we had never paid attention to but who have always lived there, with us." What kinds of trees surround you? Where does your water come from? Your heat? Your light? Your food? Where does your garbage go? What watershed do you live in? What's the phase of the moon? What's the hardiness zone? And so on and so on. These rivers, trees, birds, animals, and plants are "fundamental parts" of ourselves. How would our lives change if we truly saw the earth as alive and part of us?

More than anything, this book is a *big wake-up call.* Wake up to the world around you. See the world differently. Use all your senses, your full-bodied, enfleshed, landed location. For the crisis we face with regard to the earth is deeply cosmological and spiritual in the most embodied, material way. It is all about our limited worldview and our inhibiting world performance. Ritual practices matter deeply because capitalism has formed us deeply, more than we can even begin to imagine, leaving even the most nature-oriented among us with a view of nature as a mere "resource for development and profit." Indeed, we can't even *see* nature, believing it lies way outside our territory even though we are immersed immediately within it all the time. This objectification and exploitation is partly why Macfarlane chooses to address rivers as full beings "who" flow through the land. But to use "who" rather than "it" for rivers and trees who surround us, or to "rise, bow, and touch the ground," these bold acts of imagination and embodiment "bring forth another Spirit/s," as Cláudio insists and demonstrates. To rise, bow, and touch the ground are "practices of reimagination" and collective transformation. "We start by walking, paying attention, slowly growing familiar with and getting closer to the beings/species around us." These practices are "portals" to fall in love with the more than human. The "gestures I describe are intended to start us down that path." They involve reciprocity and responsibility, igniting and fulfilling an obligation that extends beyond the individual to the whole. "We can't just practice our ritual gestures and move on," he says. "As we start to relate to the land in which we live, we become responsible for that very land."

All this to say: *Spiritual Practices for Ecological Survival* arrived in my email inbox as a breath of fresh air from the opening quote—remember "everything that we really love was one day, the impossible"—to the final words encouraging us to "pay attention, be aware, craft a story, and care for every being that surrounds us."

Thank you, Cláudio, creative, expert practical theologian, and wise ritual leader, for once again pushing us, your readers and your followers onward. Thank you for this brave manifesto that paves a way where there so often seems to be no way through climate chaos. Thank you for sending us forth with hope and determination. You have truly revealed the earth shimmering!

ENDNOTES

1 Vladimir Safatle, *O Circuito Dos Afetos: Corpos Políticos, Desamparo e o Fim do Indivíduo* (Cosac Naify/Autêntica, 2015), 36. Kindle Edition.

2 Robin Wall Kimmerer, "Marrying Indigenous Wisdom and Scientific Knowledge: Reimagining the Human Place in Nature," Union Theological Seminary, YouTube video, 1:38:45, February 27, 2019, https://www.youtube.com/watch?v=ucNmu-WNNDk&t=5372s

3 Jeremy Narby, *The Cosmic Serpent: DNA and the Origins of Knowledge* (Tarcher, 1999), 36. Kindle Edition. Italics mine.

4 "As their torsos shrink, their wings lengthen, as if equipping them to fly toward an increasingly distant future. There is an external force, invisible and incomprehensible to these beings, that invades their bodies and may be leaving permanent marks on their genes. A force faster and more intense than the one that has been slowly and gently shaping them over time. Soon, it is possible that this new force will also alter the melody of their songs, disorienting them. Finally, it may make them disappear, one by one. Without them having a chance to defend themselves. This force is called climate collapse. And it is caused by a minority of humans, super-rich shareholders of large transnational corporations, local extractive elites, Parliaments and governments that serve them." Jaqueline Sordi, "Pássaros da Amazônia estão encolhendo para se adaptar ao colapso do clima," with Luciano Candisani (photography) and Hadna Abreu (illustrations), *Sumaúma*, February 10, 2025, https://sumauma.com/passaros-da-amazonia-estao-encolhendo-para-se-adaptar-ao-colapso-do-clima/. My translation.

5 Julia Webster Ayuso, "As mudanças climáticas estão matando palavras e línguas," *Agência Pública*, February 17, 2025, https://apublica.org/2025/02/as-mudancas-climaticas-estao-matando-palavras-e-linguas/?utm_source=instagram&utm_medium=post&utm_campaign=sami

6 Instituto Humanitas Unisinos, "COP16: Perdida da biodiversidade é a maior crise planetária. Entrevista especial com Aliny Pires," October 29, 2024, https://www.ihu.unisinos.br/645351-cop-16-perda-da-biodiversidade-e-a-maior-crise-planetaria-entrevista-especial-com-aliny-pires?utm_campaign=newsletter_ihu__29-10-2024&utm_medium=email&utm_source=RD+Station

7 Tom Perkins, "Alaska to Resume 'Barbaric' Shooting of Bears and Wolves from Helicopters," *The Guardian*, January 20, 2025, https://www.theguardian.com/us-news/2025/jan/20/alaska-aerial-gunning-bears-wolves

8 "Two-Thirds of Global Warming Caused by World's Richest 10%, Study Finds," *Al Jazeera*, May 7, 2025, https://www.aljazeera.com/news/2025/5/7/two-thirds-of-global-warming-caused-by-worlds-richest-10-study-finds

9 Johnson, "What Now for Climate."

10 Gil Anidjar, "On the Sovereignty of Mothers: The Political as Maternal," Union Theological Seminary, February 19, 2025, https://utsnyc.edu/blog/event/on-the-sovereignty-of-mothers-the-political-as-maternal/ (Unrecorded meeting.)

11 This is a popular saying in Brazil. One online instance can be found at Visibilidade Indígena—VI, "Nós não estamos defendendo a natureza. Nós somos a natureza defendendo a si mesma!" Facebook, February 6, 2019, https://www.facebook.com/visibilidadeindigena/photos/n%C3%B3s-n%C3%A3o-estamos-defendendo-a-natureza-n%C3%B3s-somos-a-natureza-defendendo-a-si-mesma/1231664720291774/

12 Paul B. Preciado, *Dysphoria Mundi: A Diary of Planetary Transition* (Graywolf Press, 2025), 21.

13 Catherine Bell, "Performance," in *Critical Terms for Religious Studies*, ed. Mark C. Taylor (University of Chicago Press, 1998), 221.

14 Join me! Cláudio Carvalhaes, "A Three Liturgical Gesture Song," YouTube video, 1:22, April 4, 2024, https://www.youtube.com/watch?v=1xxJnbkY5eQ. In Spanish: "Un triple gesto litúrgico," YouTube video, 1:19, April 12, 2024, https://www.youtube.com/watch?v=219i22TbF_Y

15 Gayraud S. Wilmore, *Pragmatic Spirituality: The Christian Faith through an Africentric Lens* (NYU Press, 2004), 40.

16 See NAACP, "Lift Every Voice and Sing," accessed March 4, 2025, https://naacp.org/find-resources/history-explained/lift-every-voice-and-sing

17 Bruno Latour, "Seven Objections against Landing on Earth," in *Critical Zones: The Science and Politics of Landing on Earth*, eds. Bruno Latour and Peter Weibel (MIT Press, 2020).

18 See Warren Dean, *A Ferro e Fogo. A história e a devastação da Mata Atlântica brasileira* (Companhia das Letras, 1996).

19 Throughout the book you will see the term *Bioregion*. The section "Bioregion and Other Terms" will describe it better. For now, we can stay with Bill Devall's description of it: "Bio means life and region means the territory or lifeworld of experience. Literally, then, a bioregion is the territory of lived experience, the territory with which a person, or a community of people, identifies as part of their self." See note 90.

20 Dipesh Chakrabarty, *The Climate of History in a Planetary Age* (University of Chicago Press, 2021).

21 Robin Wall Kimmerer, *Braiding Sweetgrass: Indigenous Wisdom, Scientific Knowledge and the Teachings of Plants* (Milkweed Editions, 2015), 36, 37, 38, Kindle Edition.

22 Kimmerer, *Braiding Sweetgrass*, 34.

23 Vinciane Despret. *Autobiografia De Um Polvo: E Outras Narrativas De Antecipação* (Bazar do Tempo, 2022), 676. Kindle Edition.

24 Félix Guattari, *Revolução Molecular Pulsações Políticas Do Desejo* (Editora Brasiliense, 1981), 205. My translation.

25 Joel Goldberg, "It Takes a Village to Determine the Origins of an African Proverb," *NPR*, July 30, 2016. https://www.npr.org/sections/goatsandsoda/2016/07/30/487925796/it-takes-a-village-to-determine-the-origins-of-an-african-proverb

26 Anna Lowenhaupt Tsing, "Arts of Inclusion, or, How to Love a Mushroom," *Australian Humanities Review* 50 (May 2011), https://australianhumanitiesreview.org/2011/05/01/arts-of-inclusion-or-how-to-love-a-mushroom/

27 Tyson Yunkaporta, *Sand Talk: How Indigenous Thinking Can Save the World* (New York: HarperOne, 2020), 1, 7, 214, 298. Kindle Edition.

28 Embassies are places of encounter where interspecies are interconnected, landscapes where many worlds of many species, humans, and more-than-human live together. To create an embassy is to be attentive to the many forms of life around us and learn how to communicate, foster, protect and enhance collective life in a certain bioregion.

29 Isabelle Stengers, *Cosmopolitics I*, trans. Robert Bononno (University of Minnesota Press, 2010), 52–53.

30 Donna Haraway, "Situated Knowledges: The Science Question in Feminism and the Privilege of Partial Perspective," *Feminist Studies* 14, no. 3 (1988): 575–599.

31 Donna Haraway, *The Companion Species Manifesto: Dogs, People, and Significant Otherness* (Prickly Paradigm Press, 2003).

32 Alexandre Nodari, "A saída para as encruzilhadas no Antropoceno está não em nós mesmos, mas em nós-outros. Entrevista especial com Alexandre Nodari," *Baleia Comunicação*, May 21, 2025, https://www.ihu.unisinos.br/652014-a-saida-para-as-encruzilhadas-no-antropoceno-esta-em-nos-mesmos-mas-em-nos-outros-entrevista-especial-com-alexandre-nodari?utm_campaign=newsletter_ihu__22-05-2025&utm_medium=email&utm_source=RD+Station

33 See: Jack D. Forbes, "Indigenous Americans: Spirituality and Ecos," in *Religion and Ecology: Can the Climate Change?*, eds. Mary Evelyn Tucker and John A. Grim (Daedalus, Fall 2001); Black Elk, *Wakan-Taka: The Great Spirit*, n.d., https://great-spirit-mother.org/; https://anishinabeknews.ca/2015/05/divergence-traditional-aboriginal-spirituality-and-mother-earth/; "Traditional Aboriginal Spirituality and Mother Earth," *Anishinabek News*, May 13, 2015. https://anishinabeknews.ca/2015/05/divergence-traditional-aboriginal-spirituality-and-mother-earth/

34 John 3:8, *New Revised Standard Version Updated Bible: With Deuterocanonical and Apocryphal Books of the Old Testament* (New Revised Standard Version Updated Edition), USA, National Council of Churches, 4116. Kindle Edition.

35 Martin Luther, in *The Reformation: A Narrative History Related by Contemporary Observers and Participants*, ed. Hans J. Hillerbrand (New York: Harper & Row, 1964), 28.

36 Bruno Latour, *An Inquiry into Modes of Existence. An Anthropology of the Moderns* (Harvard University Press, 2013), 488.

37 Eduardo Viveiros de Castro, "Colóquio Internacional- A vida enigmática dos signos: O estruturalismo dionísico e as metafísicas canibais

Literatura PUC-SP," November 12, 2024, https://www.youtube.com/watch?v=LEH_Aav7FhA&t=2495s

38 Emanuele Coccia, "Preface," in *The Spirit of the Forest*, eds. Bruce Albert and Davi Kopenawa (Companhia das Letras, 2021), 7–8. Kindle Edition.

39 *Molecular revolution* is a term you will also see frequently in this book. The term was coined by French philosopher Felix Guattari and refers to small-scale, everyday transformations in desire, subjectivity, and social relations that happen at the micro-level of life—in how we perceive, feel, think, relate to others, and organize ourselves. In this book we are fundamentally understanding it in relation with the land. The three ritual gestures offered in this book are indeed *molecular revolutions* in which they are processes of experimental, provisional actions that operate at multiple sites, bioregions, at the level of everyday life, places, desires, relationships, and subjective experience. Molecular revolutions complement, ignite, change and create macro-politics. See more in the section *Molecular Revolutions*.

40 "Attention is not lent, nor given, nor granted: it is constituted, configured, shaped. Attention is latency in the sensor interface. So the question is how to intervene there: compose with other sensors. Construct sensors and combine them in multiple ways. Paying attention to the multiplicity inscribed in the very word 'sensor' (to sense, sensing): register, detect, perceive, capture, observe. A sensor can be many things, and its compositions produce differentiated intelligences. It's no longer a question of capture, dispersion, or lack: it's about composing other interfaces." Emmanuel Biset, "Sensores De Guerra. 9 Tesis Sobre Políticas De La Atención." in *Arqueologias del porvenir*, n.d., https://arqueologiasdelporvenir.com.ar/ensayos/

41 David Abram, *The Spell of the Sensuous: Perception and Language in a More-than-Human World* (Vintage Books, 2017), 304. Kindle Edition.

42 Maurice Merleau-Ponty, *Nature: Course Notes from the Collège de France.* Compiled and with notes by Dominique Séglard (Northwestern University Press, 2003), 159.

43 Merleau-Ponty, *Nature,* XX.

44 Abram, *The Spell of the Sensuous*, 13–14.

45 Bruce Albert, and Davi Kopenawa. O Espírito Da Floresta (Companhia das Letras, 2021), 24–25. Kindle Edition.

46 Eduardo Viveiros de Castro, "Perspectivismo indígena," in *Visões do Rio Negro*, eds. B. Giovanni Ricardo and M. Antonio (Instituto Socioambiental, 2007), 84–92.

47 For more on metamorphosis, see Cláudio Carvalhaes, *How Do We Become Green People and Earth Communities?: Inventory, Metamorphoses, and Emergenc(i)es* (Barber's Son, 2023).

48 Gary Snyder, *The Practice of the Wild, Essays by Gary Snyder* (North Point Press, 1990), 26.

49 Stephan Harding, *Animate Earth-Science, Intuition and Gaia* (Green Publishing Company), 40.

50 Clarice Lispector, in Benjamin Moser, "Tesouro Bem Guardado. A Mais Abrangente Entrevista Com Clarice Lispector Resgata Seu Lado Falante

E Descontraído," *Quatro Cinco Um*, Edição #72, July 31, 2023, https://quatrocincoum.com.br/entrevistas/literatura/literatura-brasileira/tesouro-bem-guardado/

51 Cited by Snyder, *The Practice of the Wild*, 25.

52 Cláudio Carvalhaes, "Trees and Plants around My House," YouTube video, 11:18, November 9, 2021, https://www.youtube.com/watch?v=EabmuW1CZ6o&t=44s

53 See Nicole Soares Pinto, "Ecologia com espírito dentro": sobre Povos Indígenas, Xamanismo e Antropoceno, Cadernos IHUideias ISSN 1679-0316, ano 19 • nº 316 • vol. 19 • 2021, https://www.ihu.unisinos.br/categorias/608752-ecologia-com-espirito-dentro-sobre-povos-indigenas-xamanismo-e-antropoceno

54 For more on emergences and emergencies, see Carvalhaes, *How Do We Become Green People.*

55 Abram, *The Spell of the Sensuous*, 58.

56 Nancy Fraser, "Workers Are Cannibalised by the Capitalist Class: Nancy Fraser," *UpFront*, February 14, 2025, video, 24:58, https://www.aljazeera.com/program/upfront/2025/2/14/workers-are-cannibalised-by-the-capitalist-class-nancy-fraser

57 Proverbs 11:14, *The Holy Bible New Revised Standard Version Updated Bible: With Deuterocanonical and Apocryphal Books of the Old Testament*, 1956. Kindle Edition.

58 Walter Benjamin defines this religion: "A religion may be discerned in capitalism—that is to say, capitalism serves essentially to allay the same anxieties, torments, and disturbances to which the so-called religions offered answers. . . . In the first place, capitalism is a purely cultic religion, perhaps the most extreme that ever existed. In capitalism, things have no meaning only in their relationship to the cult; capitalism has no specific body of dogma, no theology. It is from this point of view that utilitarianism acquires its religious overtones. This concretization of cult is connected with a second feature of capitalism: the permanence of the cult. Capitalism is the celebration of the cult *sans reve et sans merci* [without dream or mercy]. There are no 'weekdays.' Capitalism is entirely without precedent, in that it is a religion which offers not the reform of existence but its complete destruction. It is the expansion of despair, until despair becomes a religious state of the world in the hope that this will lead to salvation." Walter Benjamin, *Selected Writings Volume 1* (Belknap Harvard Press, 1996), 288–291.

59 Augustine of Hippo, *Confessions*, trans. Gary Wills (Penguin, 2008), chapter X, page 7.

60 Matthew 6:21, *The Holy Bible.*

61 "Cio da Terra," LP Geraes, Milton Nascimento, Chico Buarque (EMI, 1976).

62 Merriam-Webster, "Beatific," last updated August 1, 2025, https://www.merriam-webster.com/dictionary/beatific

63 Deborah Bird Rose, "Shimmer When All You Love Is Being Trashed," in *Arts of Living on a Damaged Planet: Ghosts and Monsters of the Anthropocene*,

eds. Anna Lowenhaupt Tsing, Nils Bubandt, Elaine Gan, and Heather Anne Swanson (University of Minnesota Press, 2017), 909. Kindle Edition.

64 Rose, "Shimmer," 1040.

65 Rose, "Shimmer," 909.

66 Rose, "Shimmer," 909.

67 Rose, "Shimmer," 928.

68 Rose, "Shimmer," 947.

69 Despret, *Autobiografia de um Polvo*.

70 Jane Goodall, "Primate Spirituality," in *Encyclopedia of Religion and Nature*, ed. Bron Taylor (New York: Continuum, 2005), 1304.

71 James B. Harrod, "The Case for Chimpanzee Religion," *Journal for the Study of Religion, Nature and Culture*, 8, no. 1, Equinox (2014): 8.

72 Despret, *Autobiografia*, 386.

73 Harrod, "Chimpanzee Religion," 28.

74 Despret, *Autobiografia*, 386.

75 Despret, *Autobiografia*, 954.

76 Vinciane Despret, *What Would Animals Say If We Asked the Right Questions?* (University of Minnesota Press, 2016).

77 Despret, *Autobiografia*, 968.

78 "Que a importância de uma coisa há que ser medida pelo encantamento que a coisa produza em nós." Manoel Bandeira, "Sobre Importâncias," in *Obra Memórias Inventadas—A Segunda Infância* (Editora Alfaguara, 2018), 43.

79 Claude Lévi-Strauss, *The Raw and the Cooked: Introduction to a Science of Mythology*, Volume 1, trans. John and Doreen Weightman (New York: Harper & Row, 1969).

80 Richard Schechner, *The Future of Ritual: Writings on Culture and Performance* (Routledge, 1995), 20.

81 Nathan D. Mitchell, *Meeting Mystery: Liturgy, Worship, Sacraments* (Orbis Books, 2007), 59.

82 Félix Guattari and Suely Rolnik, *Molecular Revolution in Brazil* (Semiotext(e): 2008), 9.

83 Tom F. Driver, *Liberating Rites: Understanding the Transformative Power of Ritual*, 1st ed. (New York: Routledge, 1998), 185. https://doi-org.ezproxy.cul.columbia.edu/10.4324/9780429040313

84 Davi Kopenawa Yanomami, "A Mãe-Terra pede socorro. O planeta pede para que a floresta seja protegida e o povo da cidade não sabe escutar," *UOL*, December 28, 2021, https://noticias.uol.com.br/reportagens-especiais/a-mae-terra-pede-socorro---davi-kopenawa-yanomami.htm

85 Preciado, *Dysphoria Mundi*, 25.

86 See my critique of Alister McGrath's *Re-imagining Nature: The Promise of a Christian Natural Theology* (Wiley Blackwell, 2017): Cláudio Carvalhaes, "Rituals and Performances in the Anthropocene: Eco-Liturgical Liberation

Pantheologies," in *Ritual at World's End: Essays on Eco-Liturgical Liberation Theology* (Barber's Son, 2021), 108–138.

87 Fernando Silva e Silva, "A natureza, um problema para a filosofia ambiental," Ecological Issues, YouTube video, 1:25:55, August 10, 2022, https://www.youtube.com/watch?v=Kh5nLC1BP1U. Anthropologist Eduardo Viveiros de Castro explains how the Western tendency to proceed according to the binary culture/nature is quite different than the ways in which Indigenous South Americans organize their lives, in "Cosmological Deixis and Amerindian Perspectivism," *The Journal of the Royal Anthropological Institute* 4, no. 3 (1998): 469–488, jstor.org/stable/3034157

88 Anna Lowenhaupt Tsing, *The Mushroom at the End of the World: On the Possibility of Life in Capitalist Ruins* (Princeton University Press, 2015), 11. Kindle Edition.

89 Anna Lowenhaupt Tsing, Nils Bubandt, Elaine Gan and Heather Anne Swanson, eds., *Arts of Living on a Damaged Planet: Ghosts and Monsters of the Anthropocene* (University of Minnesota Press, 2017).

90 Planet Drum Foundation, "About Planet Drum Foundation," accessed August 7, 2025, https://planetdrum.org/about-us/. Italics in original.

91 Karl Burkart, "What Is a Bioregion?" OneEarth, July 26, 2024, https://www.oneearth.org/what-is-a-bioregion/

92 Anna Lowenhaupt Tsing, Andrew S. Mathews and Nils Bubandt, "Patchy Anthropocene: Landscape Structure, Multispecies History, and the Retooling of Anthropology. An Introduction to Supplement 20," *Current Anthropology* 60, no. S20, https://www.journals.uchicago.edu/doi/10.1086/703391

93 Bill Devall, *Living Deep Ecology: A Bioregional Journey* (Lexington Books, 2021), xx.

94 Kimmerer, *Braiding Sweetgrass*; Yunkaporta, *Sand Talk*; Stefano Mancuso, *The Revolutionary Genius of Plants: A New Understanding of Plant Intelligence and Behavior* (Atria Books, 2018); Carl Safina, *Beyond Words: What Animals Think and Feel* (Henry Holt, 2015); Val Plumwood, *The Eye of the Crocodile*, ed. Lorraine Shannon (The Australian National University, 2012); David Abram, *The Spell of the Sensuous*, Alexis Pauline Gumbs, *Undrowned: Black Feminist Lessons from Marine Mammals* (AK Press, 2020); Vinciane Despret and Helen Morrison, *Living as a Bird* (Polity, 2021).

95 *The New Yorker*, *How Soundscapes Change after a Fire | "The Last of the Nightingales" | The New Yorker Documentary*, YouTube video, 32:43, February 13, 2025, https://www.youtube.com/watch?v=w-0IzU1EDdk

96 Anne Bogart, *And Then, You Act: Making Art in an Unpredictable World* (Routledge, 2007), 34. Emphasis in original.

97 Bogart, *And Then, You Act*, 52.

98 Donna Haraway, *Staying with the Trouble: Making Kin in the Chthulucene* (Duke University Press, 2016).

99 Larry L. Rasmussen, *Earth-Honoring Faith: Religious Ethics in a New Key* (Oxford University Press, 2013), 334.

100 Tyson Yunkaporta, *Right Story, Wrong Story: How to Have Fearless Conversations in Hell* (HarperOne, 2023), 84–85. Kindle Edition.

101 Tsing, Mathews and Bubandt, "Patchy Anthropocene," S188.

102 Tsing, Mathews and Bubandt, "Patchy Anthropocene," S190.

103 Tsing, Mathews and Bubandt, "Patchy Anthropocene," S191.

104 Matthew 6:21, KJV.

105 Bruno Latour, *After Lockdown* (Polity, 2021), 7.

106 Latour, *After Lockdown*, 55.

107 Latour, *After Lockdown*, 48–49.

108 Latour, *After Lockdown*, 50.

109 Latour, *After Lockdown*, 51.

110 Chakrabarty, *The Climate of History in a Planetary Age*.

111 Latour, *After Lockdown*, 51.

112 Emanuele Coccia, "Prefácio," in Bruce Albert and Davi Kopenawa, *O Espírito Da Floresta* (Companhia das Letras, 2021), 13–14. Kindle Edition.

113 Coccia, "Prefácio," 17.

114 Yunkaporta, *Right Story, Wrong Story*, 87–88.

115 Three examples of bioregion quizzes can be found at Tina Fields et al, "Bioregional Awareness Quiz," *Watershed Commons*, accessed March 5, 2025, https://deptofbioregion.org/resources/bioregional-quiz/; Regenerative Design Institute, "Bioregional Quiz," accessed March 5, 2025, https://www.regenerativedesign.org/resources/documents/bioregional-quiz; and Leonard Charles, Jim Dodge, Lynn Milliman, and Victoria Stockley, "Where You At? A Bioregional Quiz," *Coevolution Quarterly* 32 (1981): 1, https://dces.wisc.edu/wp-content/uploads/sites/128/2013/08/Where-You-At-Quiz.pdf. The quiz here was informed by all three listed here.

116 Vitor Westhelle, *Eschatology and Space: The Lost Dimension in Theology Past and Present* (Palgrave Macmillan, 2012), 8. Kindle Edition.

117 "Colere, to cultivate," Allo Latin, last modified September 26, 2023, https://ancientlanguages.org/latin/dictionary/colo-colere-colui-cultum#:~:text=col%C5%8D%2C%20colere%2C%20colu%C4%AB%2C%20cultum,Definitions%20for%20colere

118 Alfredo Bosi, *Brazil and the Dialectic of Colonization*, trans. Robert Patrick Newcomb (University of Illinois Press, 2015), 124. Kindle Edition.

119 Marcelo Leite, "Bolsonaro derruba até 1 bilhão de árvores na Amazônia em 12 meses," *Folha de São Paulo*, November 22, 2021, https://www.ihu.unisinos.br/categorias/614651-bolsonaro-derruba-ate-1-bilhao-de-arvores-na-amazonia-em-12-meses-frases-do-dia

120 Aimé Césaire, *Discourse on Colonialism*, trans. John Pinkham (Monthly Review Press, 2001), 32–33. Kindle Edition.

121 G. W. F. Hegel, *Encyclopedia of the Philosophical Sciences, Part II: Philosophy of Nature*, trans. A. W. Miller (Clarendon Press, 2004), 34.

122 Westhelle, *Eschatology and Space*, 11.

123 Jonathan Z. Smith, *To Take Place: Toward Theory in Ritual* (Chicago: University of Chicago Press, 1987), 114.

124 Michel de Certeau, *The Practice of Everyday Life*, trans. Steven Rendall (University of California Press, 1984), 117.

125 John 15:19, NRSV.

126 Eduardo Viveiros de Castro, "Prefácio," in *A queda do céu: Palavras de um xamã yanomami*, eds. Davi Kopenawa and Bruce Albert, trans. Beatriz Perrone-Moisés (Companhia das Letras, 2015), 5. My translation.

127 Tyson Yunkaporta, "Deep Time Diligence, a Conversation with Tyson Yunkaporta," in *Emerging Magazine Podcast*, February 11, 2025.

128 Marisol de la Cadena, "An Invitation to Live Together: Making the 'Complex We,'" *Environmental Humanities* 11, no. 2 (2019): 477–484. https://doi.org/10.1215/22011919-7754589; https://read.dukeupress.edu/environmental-humanities/article/11/2/477/140789/An-Invitation-to-Live-TogetherMaking-the-Complex

129 de la Cadena, "An Invitation to Live Together."

130 María Puig de la Bellacasa, *Matters of Care. Speculative Ethics in More than Human Worlds* (University of Minnesota Press, 2017).

131 "One Does Not Live by Bread Alone, but by Every Word that Comes from the Mouthof God." Matthew 4:4, NRSV.

132 Westhelle, *Eschatology and Space*, 8.

133 Mark I. Wallace, *When God Was a Bird: Christianity, Animism, and the Re-Enchantment of the World* (Fordham University Press, 2019), 33. Kindle Edition.

134 Smith, *To Take Place*, 103.

135 Smith, *To Take Place*, 76–95, 115–16.

136 Ronald Grimes, *The Craft of Ritual Studies* (Oxford University Press, 2013), 256–59.

137 Vitória Régia da Silva, "Na primeira March das Mulheres Indígenas, território, corpo e identidade estão no centro do discurso," *Gênero e Número*, August 8, 2019, https://www.generonumero.media/reportagens/marcha-mulheres-indigenas/

138 Haraway, "Situated Knowledges," 591, 595.

139 Vine Deloria Jr., "Sacred Lands and Religious Freedom," *Sacred Land Film Project*, 1, accessed March 18, 2025, https://sacredland.org/wp-content/PDFs/SacredLandReligiousFreedom.pdf

140 Deloria Jr., "Sacred Lands and Religious Freedom," 3.

141 Ronald L. Grimes, "Ritual Theory and the Environment," *The Sociological Review* 51, no. 2 (2003): 33.

142 Grimes, "Ritual Theory," 31.

143 Fernando Pessoa, "Ela canta, pobre ceifeira," *Poesias* (Ática, 1995), 108. My translation.

144 Adauto Novaes, "A Sensibilidade e a Construção do Mundo," *Mutações*, January 2024, https://www.generonumero.media/reportagens/marcha-mulheres-indigenas/. My translation.

145 Ronald L. Grimes, "Reinventing Ritual," *Soundings: An Interdisciplinary Journal* 75, no. 1 (1992): 22.

146 Jon Batiste, "The Musical Genius of Jon Batiste," posted November 4, 2024, by Tim Ferriss, YouTube, 13:58, https://www.youtube.com/watch?v=wjthOKE8rcE

147 Grimes, "Reinventing Ritual," 22.

148 Ronald L. Grimes, "A Sense for Ritual," *Circling the Deep*, February 27, 2024, https://circle.twohornedbull.ca/a-sense-for-ritual/

149 Grimes, "Ritual Theory and the Environment," 44.

150 "Corporate branding is the cultural mechanism through which capitalism has iteratively extended its sacred power in the neoliberal period, especially in the past thirty years. Brands invite consumers to participate in self- and world-making rituals that press particular values, priorities, and ways of seeing upon us." George González, *The Church of Stop Shopping and Religious Activism: Combatting Consumerism and Climate Change through Performance* (NYU Press, 2024), 35.

151 Ernest Dichter cited in González, *The Church of Stop Shopping*, 63.

152 Giambattista Vico, *The New Science*, trans. Jason Taylor and Robert C. Miner (Yale University Press, 2020), 148.

153 John 10:10, NRSV.

154 The 1.5°C target comes from the 2015 Paris Agreement, where 196 countries committed to limiting global temperature rise to well below 2°C above pre-industrial levels while pursuing efforts to limit the temperature increase to 1.5°C. 2°C would dramatically worsen climate impacts—including doubled risk to water stress for billions of people, significantly more species extinctions, and the near-total loss of coral reefs. However, current commitments fall far short: we're on track for approximately 2.7–3°C of warming by 2100, making the 1.5°C target increasingly difficult to achieve without immediate, dramatic reductions in greenhouse gas emissions across all sectors globally. See IPCC, Global Warming of 1.5°C: Special Report (Geneva: IPCC, 2018).

155 Daniel Augusto, interview with Eduardo Viveiros de Castro, *Incertezas Críticas*, season 3, 2021. Online video, 26:00, 2021, https://tamandua.tv.br/filme/default.aspx?name=eduardo-viveiros-de-castro1#. My translation.

156 Augusto, *Incertezas Críticas*.

157 Abraham Joshua Heschel, "On Prayer," *Conservative Judaism* 25, no. 1 (1970): 5, https://archive.org/details/OnPrayerAbrahamJoshuaHeschel1969/page/n3/mode/2up

158 Thich Nhat Hanh, "The Insight of Interbeing," *Garrison Institute*, August 2, 2017, https://www.garrisoninstitute.org/insight-of-interbeing/

159 Davi Kopenawa, "The Yanomami Struggle," *The Institute of Latin American Studies*, Columbia University, February 3, 2023, https://ilas.columbia.edu/events/yanomami-struggle-davi-kopenawa

160 Ada Limón, ed. *You Are Here: Poetry in the Natural World* (Milkweed Editions, 2024), 3.

161 See Kimmerer, *Braiding Sweetgrass.*

162 Heschel, "On Prayer," 3.

163 Heschel, "On Prayer," 2.

164 Kimmerer, *Braiding Sweetgrass.*

165 Ram Dass defines witness consciousness this way: "The witness is actually another level of consciousness. The witness coexists alongside your normal consciousness as another layer of awareness, as the part of you that is awakening. Humans have this unique ability to be in two states of consciousness at once. Witnessing yourself is like directing the beam of a flashlight back at itself. In any experience—sensory, emotional, or conceptual—there's the experience, the sensory or emotional or thought data, and there's your awareness of it. That's the witness, the awareness, and you can cultivate that awareness in the garden of your being." Ram Dass with Rameshwar Das, *Polishing the Mirror: How to Live from Your Spiritual Heart* (Sounds True, 2013), 124.

166 Heschel, "On Prayer," 2.

167 Heschel, "On Prayer," 263.

168 Kimmerer, *Braiding Sweetgrass*, 24–26.

169 Wendell Berry, "Forward," in *Of the Land & the Spirit. The Essential Lord Northbourne on Ecology & Religion*, eds. Christopher James and Joseph A. Fitzgerald (World Wisdom, 2008), viii.

170 Wendell Berry, *Given New Poems* (Counterpoint, 2005), 18.

171 Félix Guattari, *A Revolução Molecular*, translated by Larissa Drigo Agostinho (Ubu Editora, 2024), 23.

172 Antonio Bispo dos Santos, *A Terra Dá, A Terra Quer* (Piseagrama, Ubu, 2023), 69, Kindle Edition.

173 Nêgo Bispo, "Começo, Meio e Começo," *Revista Revestres* 25 de abril de 2025, https://revistarevestres.com.br/entrevista/comeco-meio-e-comeco/

174 Leda Maria Martins, *Performances of Spiral Time* (Duke University Press, 2025), 105.

175 Kimmerer, *Braiding Sweetgrass*, 16.

176 Felix Guattari, *Molecular Revolution: Psychiatry and Politics* (Penguin, 1984); and Guattari, A Revolução Molecular.

177 Guattari and Rolnik, *Molecular Revolution in Brazil*, 36.

178 Guattari and Rolnik, *Molecular Revolution in Brazil*, 318.

179 Félix Guattari, "Félix Guattari e a revolução molecular," Ubu Editora, YouTube vídeo, 1:35, April 24, 2024, https://www.youtube.com/watch?v=6_B6nztx1Ns

180 Rita Segato, *Contra-Pedagogías de la Crueldad* (Prometeo Editorial, 2018), 4–5.

181 So many varieties of Indigenous Knowledge employ this form of vision. See Ailton Krenak, *Ancestral Future (Critical South)* (Polity, 2024); and Santos, *A*

Terra Dá, A Terra Quer. A similar argument, although not developed in terms of a relationship with the natural world, is made by Jean-Luc Nancy, *Being Singular Plural* (Stanford University Press, 2000).

182 Félix Guattari, *The Lines of Flight. For Another World of Possibilities* (Bloomsbury Academic, 2015), 65.

183 Andrea Muehlebach, "Time of Monsters," *Society for Cultural Anthropology*, October 27, 2016, https://culanth.org/fieldsights/time-of-monsters

184 Hartmut Rosa, *The Uncontrollability of the World* (Polity, 2020), viii–ix. Kindle Edition.

185 Rosa, *The Uncontrollability of the World*, viii–ix.

186 Preciado, *Dysphoria Mundi*, 35.

187 See Gilles Deleuze, *Pure Immanence: Essays on a Life* (MIT Press, 2005).

188 Joerg Rieger, *Theology in the Capitalocene: Ecology, Identity, Class, and Solidarity* (Fortress Press, 2022), 73.

189 Rubem Alves, *Poet, the Warrior, the Prophet* (Westminster John Knox, 2002).

190 González, *The Church of Stop Shopping*..

191 Jean Tible, *Política Selvagem* (N-1 Edições, 2022).

192 Tible, *Política Selvagem*, 181.

193 Latour reminds us that the division between human and nonhuman "has now become 'superfluous, immoral and—to put it bluntly—anti-Constitutional.'" The Parliament of things, even if with its own criticisms, has a great way to awaken in us the fact that we must find a way to hear every form of life for every form of life matters: "we should take up the two representations and the double doubt about the faithfulness of the representatives… In its confines, the continuity of the collective is reconfigured. Natures are present, but with their representatives, scientists who speak in their name. Societies are present, but with the objects that have been serving as their ballast from time immemorial." Bruno Latour, *We Have Never Been Modern* (Harvard University Press, 1993), 142–144.

194 Ailton Krenak, "Ecologia Política," Ethnoscientia, v. 3, n. 2 (2018) (ed. especial), p. 1–2.

195 Isabelle Stengers, *Cosmopolitics I* (University of Minnesota Press, 2010) and *Cosmopolitics II* (University of Minnesota Press, 2011).

196 Paulo Freire, *Pedagogy of the Oppressed*, 50th Anniversary Edition (Bloomsbury Academic, 2018), 87.

197 Eduardo Viveiros de Castro, "A luta contra o fascismo na Era do colapso global (com Safatle, Viveiros de Castro e Dani Balbi)," Tarcísio Motta, YouTube video, 2:13:08, July 7, 2024, https://www.youtube.com/watch?v=eR9x3eflyvc

198 See citations of notes 5 and 24.

199 See Karl Marx, *Capital*, Volume 3 (Vintage Books, 1981).

200 Lior Greenspoon, Eyal Krieger and Ron Sender, et al., "The Global Biomass of Wild Mammals," *Proceedings of the National Academy of Sciences of the United States of America* 120, no. 10 (2023). https://www.pnas.org/doi/10.1073/pnas.2204892120

201 See, for example, the contrast Isabelle Stengers makes between progress and gratitude: *Magic and Ecology Insurrection Interviews Podcast*, episode 3, Center for Research in the Arts, Social Sciences and Humanities, YouTube 1:31:54, December 16, 2020, https://www.youtube.com/watch?v=N8IALHq_Kcs. See also Antônio Bispo dos Santos's discussion of development as detachment from the land: "We Belong to the Land. Insights from a Quilombola Thinker on Brazil's State-Sanctioned Violence and the Power of Oral Traditions," *Futuress*, April 12, 2023, https://futuress.org/stories/we-belong-to-the-land/; and Kohei Saito, *Slow Down: The Degrowth Manifesto* (Astra House, 2024).

202 Russell Means, "For America to Live, Europe Must Die," *blackhawkproductions*.com, accessed February 18, 2025, https://blackhawkproductions.com/russelmeans.html

203 Bayard Johnson and Russell Means, *If You've Forgotten the Names of the Clouds, You've Lost Your Way: An Introduction to American Indian Thought and Philosophy* (BookBaby, 2013), 25. Kindle Edition.

204 Krenak, *Ancestral Future*, 71–72. Kindle Edition.

205 Westhelle, *Eschatology and Space*, 6.

206 "As in walking, imagine that in this type of path, the initial form of the topological-relational surface of the world is multiplied and differentiated, in a continuous process of composition and recomposition. In this micropolitics, the actions of desire therefore consist of acts of creation that are inscribed in the established existential territories and their respective cartographies, breaking the peaceful scene of the instituted." Suely Rolnik, *Esferas da insurreição* (n-1 edições), 46. Kindle Edition. My translation.

207 Giorgio Agamben, "Notas Sobre o Gesto," trans. Vinícius Nicastro, *Artefilosofia* 3 no. 4 (2008): 10. My translation.

208 Thich Nhat Hanh, "I Have Arrived," posted July 24, 2024, Plum Village App, YouTube, 5:02, https://youtu.be/qRksCEvJv20?si=7Zv6RYhI6IDGJGdF

209 Anonymous student, "Meditations," class assignment for *Sacraments, Ecology, Hospitality, and Globalization-CW 223*, Union Theological Seminary, Spring 2025.

210 Isabelle Stengers, "The Cosmopolitical Proposal," in *Making Things Public: Atmospheres of Democracy*, eds. Bruno Latour and Peter Weibel (MIT Press), 994.

211 See note 120: Guattari, "Félix Guattari e a revolução molecular."

212 Rieger, *Theology in the Capitalocene*, 67.

213 Rob R. Dunn, *Never Home Alone: From Microbes to Millipedes, Camel Crickets, and Honeybees, the Natural History of Where We Live* (New York: Basic Books, 2018), 2. Kindle Edition.

214 Thor Hanson, *Close to Home: The Wonders of Nature Just Outside Your Door* (New York: Basic Books, 2025), 213. Kindle Edition.

215 Patrick Marques, "Movimento busca ajudar no reflorestamento de comunidades tradicionais da Amazônia," *G1*, November 04, 2021, https://g1.globo.com/am/amazonas/natureza/amazonia/noticia/2021/11/04/

movimento-busca-ajudar-no-reflorestamento-de-comunidades-tradicionais-da-amazonia.ghtml

216 Editors, "Quando os cidadãos se unem para mudar os seus bairros," *Diário de Notícias*, August 30, 2017, https://www.dn.pt/sociedade/quando-os-cidadaos-se-unem-para-mudar-os-seus-bairros-8738887.html

217 Alliance and the Chesapeake Bay, Conodoguinet Creek Watershed Association.

218 All efforts mentioned in this paragraph up to this point are discussed in "5 iniciativas internacionais de restauração florestal e o que elas podem ensinar ao Brasil," June 10, 2019, https://www.wribrasil.org.br/noticias/5-iniciativas-internacionais-de-restauracao-florestal-e-o-que-elas-podem-ensinar-ao-brasil. My translation

219 UN Environment Programme, "On World Cities Day, UNEP Announces 19 Cities to Restore Nature's Rightful Place in Urban Areas," October 31, 2023, https://www.unep.org/technical-highlight/world-cities-day-unep-announces-19-cities-restore-natures-rightful-place-urban

220 Safiya Rebhi, "Meditations," class assignment for *Introduction to Ritual/Worship-CW 103*, Union Theological Seminary, September 28, 2025.

221 Robin Wall Kimmerer, *The Serviceberry: Abundance and Reciprocity in the Natural World* (Scribner, 2024).

222 Melanie Baker, "Meditations," class assignment for *Sacraments, Ecology, Hospitality, and Globalization-CW 223*, Union Theological Seminary in New York, Spring 2025.

223 Melissa Bellew, "Meditations," class assignment for *Sacraments, Ecology, Hospitality, and Globalization-CW 223*, Union Theological Seminary, April 28, 2025.

224 Driver, *Liberating Rites*, 74.

225 Spencer Williams, "Meditations," class assignment for *CW 247–Liturgies from Below: Prayers in Defiance of Empire*, Union Theological Seminary, June 2024.

226 Ed Shanahan, "Flaco, Escaped Central Park Zoo Owl and Defier of Doubts, Is Dead," *The New York Times*, February 23, 2024, https://www.nytimes.com/2024/02/23/nyregion/flaco-owl-central-park-zoo-dead.html

227 To read more about Flaco, see David Gessner, *The Book of Flaco: The World's Most Famous Bird* (Durham: Blair, 2025); Jacqueline Emery and David Lei, *Finding Flaco: One Year with New York City's Beloved Owl* (New York: Owls of New York, 2024); Michiko Kakutani, "Escaped Owl: But Why, Exactly?" *New York Times*, March 3, 2023, https://www.nytimes.com/2023/03/03/nyregion/flaco-owl-central-park-nyc.html

228 Jonathan Hollinsworth, "The Legacy of Flaco: Finally His Own Owl," in *Flaco: The Owl Who Escaped Captivity and Won the Hearts of the World*, ed. Jonathan Hollinsworth (New York: Blurring Books, 2025).

229 Buildings, Mayor's Office of Climate and Environmental Justice. https://climate.cityofnewyork.us/subtopics/buildings/#:~:text=With%20over%201%20Million%20buildings,buildings%20more%20efficient%20and%20resilient

230 Victoria Bekiempis, "Fears New York Buildings' Deadly Toll on Migratory Birds Could Be on the Rise," *The Guardian,* November 10, 2024, https://www.theguardian.com/us-news/2024/nov/10/birds-building-collisions-new-york-city

231 Fahim Amir, *Being and Swine: The End of Nature (As We Knew It)*, (Between the Lines, 2020), 36, Kindle Edition.

232 Yunkaporta, *Sand Talk,* 51.

233 Brad Hoylman-Sigal, *Legislators, Advocates Rename Statewide Bird Safe Buildings Act the "FLACO Act,"* February 26, 2024, https://www.nysenate.gov/newsroom/press-releases/2024/brad-hoylman-sigal/legislators-advocates-rename-statewide-bird-safe

234 The New York Historical, "The Year of Flaco," accessed May 30, 2025, https://www.nyhistory.org/exhibitions/the-year-of-flaco

235 In developments similar to those of Flaco's escape, coyotes are appearing in San Francisco, and the capybaras in cities throughout Argentina and Brazil. See Heather Knight and Loren Elliott, "The Coyotes of San Francisco," *The New York Times*, May 29, 2025, https://www.nytimes.com/2025/05/19/us/coyotes-san-francisco-california.html?utm_campaign=likeshopme&utm_content=ig-nytimes&utm_medium=instagram&utm_source=dash+hudson; Jack Nicas, "Hundreds of Giant Rodents 'Conquered' This Town. Now What?" *The New York Times*, April 17, 2025, https://www.nytimes.com/2025/04/17/world/americas/argentina-capybaras-vasectomies.html; Paulo Augusto, "Por que existem tantas capivaras vivendo nas cidades?" *Terra da Gente*, June 13, 2023, https://g1.globo.com/sp/campinas-regiao/terra-da-gente/noticia/2023/06/13/por-que-existem-tantas-capivaras-vivendo-nas-cidades.ghtml

236 Ed Shanahan, "New York Mourns Flaco, an Owl Who Inspired as He Made the City His Own," *New York Times*, February 24, 2024, https://www.nytimes.com/2024/02/24/nyregion/flaco-eurasian-eagle-owl-nyc.html

237 Preciado, *Dysphoria Mundi*, 23.

238 Cláudio Carvalhaes, *Ritual at World's End: Essays on Eco-Liturgical Liberation Theology* (Barber's Son, 2021).

239 "By the Rivers of Babylon—There We Sat Down and There We Wept." Psalm 137, NRSV.

240 Oliver Milman, "Oceans Face 'Triple Threat' of Extreme Heat, Oxygen Loss and Acidification," *The Guardian*, June 4, 2024, https://www.theguardian.com/environment/article/2024/jun/04/extreme-heat-oceans-acidification

241 Octavia E. Butler, *Parable of the Sower* (Grand Central Publishing, 2023), 2. Kindle Edition.

242 Tsing, *The Mushroom at the End of the World*, 28.

243 George E. "Tink" Tinker, *American Indian Liberation: A Theology of Sovereignty* (Orbis, 2008).

INDEX